MARY of
MAGDALA

MARY of MAGDALA

REVISITING THE SOURCES

Marinella Perroni
and
Cristina Simonelli

Translated by Demetrio S. Yocum

Paulist Press
New York / Mahwah, NJ

Cover image by MoinMoin / shutterstock.com
Cover and book design by Sharyn Banks

Original title: *Maria de Magdala, una genealogia apostolica.* First published in Italy by Arcane Editrice int.le S.r.l.
World Rights: copyright © 2017, INSTITUTO MISSIONÁRIO FILHAS DE SÃO PAULO—PAULINAS EDITORA, Rua Francisco Salgado Zenha, 11, 2685-332 Prior Velho, Portugal. www.paulinas.pt.
English translation copyright © 2019 by Paulist Press

Library of Congress Cataloging-in-Publication Data
Names: Perroni, Marinella, author. | Simonelli, Cristina, author. | Yocum, Demetrio S., translator.
Title: Mary of Magdala : revisiting the sources / Marinella Perroni and Cristina Simonelli ; translated by Demetrio S. Yocum.
Other titles: Maria de Magdala. English
Description: New York, NY : Paulist Press, [2019] | "Original title: Maria de Magdala, una genealogia apostolica. First published in Italy by Arcane Editrice int.le S.r.l." | Includes bibliographical references.
Identifiers: LCCN 2018026553 (print) | LCCN 2018041082 (ebook) | ISBN 9781587688027 (ebook) | ISBN 9780809154210 (pbk. : alk. paper)
Subjects: LCSH: Mary Magdalene, Saint. | Christian women saints—Biography. | Feminism—Religious aspects—Catholic Church. | Women in Christianity—History—Early church, ca. 30–600.
Classification: LCC BS2485 (ebook) | LCC BS2485 .P4613 2019 (print) | DDC 226/.092—dc23
LC record available at https://lccn.loc.gov/2018026553

ISBN 978-0-8091-5421-0 (paperback)
ISBN 978-1-58768-802-7 (e-book)

Published by Paulist Press
997 Macarthur Boulevard
Mahwah, NJ 07430
www.paulistpress.com

Printed and bound in the United States of America

Contents

Introduction

Mary Magdalene and
the Valley of the Fairies

May you, our sister, become thousands of myriads;
may your offspring gain possession of the gates of their foes.

Genesis 24:60—Jewish blessing

The inhabitants of the mountain overlooking Reggio Emilia preserve a particular memory: they call it "the valley of the fairies," in
which they say were women's hermitages. The memory of Mary
Magdalene is celebrated in this valley. There are fairies, witches,
saints, hermits—women, finally—in a genealogical line whose symbolic strength challenges the simple sequence of chronicles. There
are wide gaps in the connections between these symbolic bonds
and concrete names and events that can be dated, but it is possible
to highlight the strength of a tradition to establish a genealogy,
even when it is not possible to retrace the whole path.

To reconstruct this kind of sequence would mean to trace the
history of at least half of Europe, looking for memories from those
almost buried in the above-mentioned valley to the famous Saint
Marys of Provence: on one hand, this is an enormous task, yet on
the other, it is one already begun in so much literature, particularly
feminist, of the last decades. We propose simply to place in this
perspective some pieces of the mosaic: those that are the most
ancient writings that the churches have laid out as the foundation
of the faith professed down the centuries, that is, the Gospels of
Matthew, Mark, Luke, and John, but also those handed down in the
form of a "genealogy of Mary" from writings dating between the

second and the fourth centuries, including the very short *Gospel of Mary* and the complex *Pistis Sofia*, often referred to as "apocryphal."

We will see to what extent these pieces present Mary to us "in flesh and bone." What relates to her in both traditions raises interesting questions: The paths that refer to Mary are not very different from those of Peter, Paul, or John at the start. So why, despite their powerful ideals and symbolic strength, do they have large interruptions, like those referring to Thomas or Philip? Why in the canonical Gospels does Mary Magdalene go from being first apostle of the resurrection to being a former prostitute, while the Gnostic texts present a ministerial conflict led by Peter against her?

We would be very naive, in the present state of the documentation at our disposal, to think we can answer these questions. Often, the power of a text lies precisely in the questions it poses— and perhaps leaves open—so that it continues to make us think and authorize other traditions. And rebuild genealogies.

Marinella Perroni and Cristina Simonelli

July 22, 2015, Memorial of Mary Magdalene

PART I

AN APOSTLE WITHOUT A STORY

❧ The Canonical Tradition ❧

MARINELLA PERRONI

Chapter I

The State of Affairs

In 1975, I was a guest, along with a Jesuit priest, of the Laisamis mission in the Marsabit Desert. One evening, the leaders of the seminomadic tribes visited the mission to welcome the two Italian visitors. Crouched on their knees, they held in their hands the symbols of their power, small and poor insignia, whose symbolic value to them was no different from that of the crown of England. Before eating the meat prepared over the fire, we watched a local catechist's presentation of the story of the passion, death, and resurrection of Jesus of Nazareth as an Italian missionary translated for the guests. At every turn of the story, the chiefs would spit on the ground: it was their way of assenting. At the betrayal in the Garden of Gethsemane, the catechist related that Jesus was betrayed with a kiss by a woman named Mary Magdalene. The elders spit on the ground. I was a bit disturbed. Later, the missionary tranquilly explained to me that it was no time to split hairs, that the important thing was that Jesus had been betrayed and not who had betrayed him. I have never forgotten it, especially during the long years of my biblical-theological formation. After all, even ancient Christian writers, or the fathers of the church, did not split hairs: Ephrem the Syrian repeatedly confused Mary, the mother of Jesus, with Mary Magdalene,[1] and Hippolytus believed the women at the tomb were Martha and Mary.[2]

It is true, from a theological point of view, that what matters is that Jesus was betrayed by one of his disciples. But is it so irrelevant to give a face and voice to each of the various characters in the Gospel narratives? Above all, is it pointless to ask which of them are only rhetorical constructs that function in the plot development of the narrative, and which ones instead are in the texts as precise testimonies of the historicity of the story of the prophet of Nazareth? If it is true, as St. Paul puts it, that we are saved by the proclamation

3

of the death and resurrection of Christ, it is also true that a keryg-matic theory such as Paul's can dangerously approach myth if it is not firmly anchored in the history of the Nazarene and of those who saw him, listened to him, and followed him.

The antidote to this dangerous leap into myth obviously has nothing to do with considering all the characters, episodes, and situations mentioned in the Gospels as historical; unfortunately, this is typical of an equally dangerous and hard-to-avoid Christian apologetic. Historical memory is such, and has value, only if it can be critically verified. Giving importance to all the historical traces present in the Gospels—regardless how few there are and how dif-ficult they are to interpret—does not grant anything to precritical naivete or positivist nostalgia, but rather attests to one's commit-ment to one's religious tradition and ecclesial community. For this reason, I devoted myself to a study of the canonical traditions on this particular female disciple of Jesus. Evidence about her is in all four canonical Gospels, and it allows us to present the figure of Mary of Magdala following the articulation of the Christian kerygma as it is preserved in the ancient formula that Paul relates in 1 Corin-thians 15:3ff. My choice seemed appropriate for two reasons: one related to content, the other to controversy.

It is worth noting in that formula that the proclamation of faith finds its most complete synthesis in the juxtaposition of two pairs of verbs: *died/ was buried* (ἀπέθανεν/ἐτάφη) and *he resurrected/ appeared* (ἐγήγερται/ὤφθη).

This same diptych provides the narrative structure to the four evangelical accounts of the passion. In both its synthetic version of the formula of faith and in the one developed as a narration, the first Christian preaching was based on these two pillars: death-burial, resurrection-apparitions. One must notice, however, that although Mary of Magdala is not mentioned in the list of appari-tions that accompany the formula of 1 Corinthians 15, in the Synoptic accounts of the passion, she instead, together with other women, plays a significant role in the development of the Easter events; and in the Fourth Gospel, she receives the first manifesta-tion of the Risen One (John 20:1–18; see Mark 16:9). Why?

The question was already present at the beginning of the Christian tradition, most likely because it was not easy to accept that

4

women were the first to receive the announcement of the resurrection, and that the first and only one present to receive an individual apparition of the Risen Lord was a woman.[3] Is this why Mary is not included in the apostolic genealogy of 1 Corinthians 15:3ff.?

It is almost impossible to propose a completely convincing solution to this problem. However, it is at least desirable that we not address the theme of primitive Christian kerygmatic preaching without clearly understanding that the different traditions developed separately from one another and intersected only later. They should clearly show signs of a certain uneasiness that has accompanied the tradition of the female disciples as protagonists. True, in all four Gospels the Easter apparition of the angel is addressed to the women. In Matthew, they are the first to worship the Risen One (28:8–10), and in John, Mary is the recipient of the Risen Lord's first manifestation. However, in Luke the eleven apostles and others considered the first announcement of the resurrection to Mary of Magdala and the others an "idle tale" (24:11). Cleopas, one of the two disciples on the road to Emmaus, says that "some women of our group astounded us...and told us that they had indeed seen a vision of angels who said that he was alive" (Luke 24:22–23). Even in Mark's ending, it is evident that the reaction to Mary's announcement is disbelief (16:11). Are the first symptoms of that process that will lead to the elimination of Mary of Magdala from the primitive apostolic genealogy already present in the canonical traditions? Although the texts cannot be read in a linear sequence, it is nevertheless a fact that 1 Corinthians 15:5 states that, first, the Risen One "appeared to Cephas, then to the twelve."

The interpretation of the New Testament writings cannot therefore disregard both sides of the problem: What was at the origin of faith in the resurrection, and what did disbelief and judgment of the women's witness as an "idle tale" mean to the emerging Christian tradition? The figure of Mary of Magdala stands out at the center.

I think that it can be said with certainty that whoever elaborated the kerygmatic formula repeated by Paul in 1 Corinthians 15:3ff., whoever incorporated it in the liturgy and transmitted it in the catechesis to Paul himself, if that person had known the primitive traditions of Jesus's death and resurrection that were the basis of the passion narratives, could have and perhaps should have said, "I confess that Christ died for our sins according to the Scriptures and that he was buried and that he rose on the third day according to the Scriptures and that he appeared to Mary of Magdala and then to the Twelve." If that was not done, it is because soon the image of the Galilean female disciple, the first witness to the death and resurrection of Jesus of Nazareth, was deprived of strength and value. Because it was not done, the story of women in the Christian church, along with that of Mary of Magdala, was diminished.

In-depth analyses are left to the readers. The bibliography on Mary of Magdala is vast and diverse.[4] Of what I have read, it is enough for me to gratefully recall the work of male and female colleagues who over the last few decades have studied with great competence the question of the historical figure, the narrative character, and the theological characterization of Mary of Magdala. From their work I draw much more than the few references made in my text.

I must first mention two articles, one by François Bovon,[5] and the other by Martin Hengel,[6] which should become part of the formation of any scholar or student because, though dated, they offer a safe starting point for any further analysis or reflection. Among other things, both debunk the belief that seeing Mary of Magdala as a historical disciple of Jesus and recipient of his first Easter appearance is a finding and claim of feminist exegetes.

A historical debt must then be recognized in two works pioneering at the time, especially in the Italian context. In 1991, Carla Ricci published a volume that derived from a thesis presented at the University of Bologna with Mauro Pesce, titled *Maria di Magdala e le molte altre. Donne sul cammino di Gesù* (Mary of Magdala and the many others: Women on the path of Jesus),[7] which has the merit of pursuing research on a strictly philological basis, but accompanied by an *e silentio* exegesis that aims to give importance not only to what is said, but also to what is left unsaid, especially regarding women. Shortly afterward, the work of Lilia Sebastiani's *Transfigurazione. Il personaggio evangelico di Maria di Magdala e il mito della peccatrice nella tradizione occidentale* came out.[8] For the first time, it brought to the attention of the mainstream Italian public the manipulation of the ecclesiastical tradition that turned the female disciple of Jesus into the penitent sinner.

Recently, however, two other fundamental studies have appeared. Meticulous and in-depth investigations by Susanne Ruschmann and Andrea Taschl-Erber have focused on the story of John's passion narrative, but at the same time they also cover with great erudition the various areas where interest in Mary of Magdala has emerged. These two monographs honor the recent exegetical research by women: the first, *Maria von Magdala: Jüngerin, Apostolin, Glaubensvorbild,*[9] and the second, *Maria von Magdalaerste Apostolin? John 20.1–18 Tradition und Relecture.*[10]

Previously, Mary R. Thompson, with *Mary of Magdala: Apostle and Leader,*[11] had already focused on the heart of the matter because she adhered to the texts with the correctness required for a critical consideration of the sources. Silke Petersen has also presented a good overall synthesis of the biblical, apocryphal, and patristic tradition of Mary's character in *Maria aus Magdala. Die Jüngerin, die Jesus liebte.*[12] The fact that these books are not available in Italian has further convinced me to dedicate myself to this book. However, it should be said that just before this volume went to press, a new publication in Italian has come out on Mary of Magdala by Valentina Alberici, titled *La chiamavano Maddalena. La donna che per prima incontrò il Risorto.*[13] Alberici follows my own path, and this is a cause of satisfaction rather than frustration for me because it shows that finally, even in Italy, it is now part of a shared intellectual capital to talk about Mary Magdalene while knowing how to distinguish among levels of tradition that have made the female disciple of Jesus into something other than what the evangelical accounts attest.

Since it deserves careful critical investigation, the patristic reception of the Gospel texts on Mary of Magdala is beyond the scope of this study. Nevertheless, I consider it appropriate to refer to it because the history of the effects of the texts on the female disciple of Jesus and on the first witness of the Risen Christ often contributes by shedding light on the same Gospel witnesses themselves. In this regard, I found the summary prepared by Elena Giannarelli particularly helpful.[14]

Then there is a text that I cannot help mentioning. It is what I would call an "unknown" book: it is impossible to find it in the libraries of Rome's theological faculties. But it contains important suggestions. Even the title is thought-provoking: *L'invenzione di Maria Maddalena*.[15] The author, Pierre-Emanuel Dauzat, knows the ancient patristic and medieval tradition very well, and knows how both have contributed to a number of legends about this woman who strongly influenced the history of Christian spirituality and art. For the understanding of the character of the Magdalene, he introduces the idea of an "embodied concept" made into a woman.[16] Although I do not agree with several of his statements, I recognize that the development of his thought requires us to seriously address the question of the tension between person and character, which is particularly decisive not only for Mary of Magdala of the later Christian tradition, but also for that of the canonical and Gnostic texts.

To Mercedes Navarro, I am much more indebted. In addition to an important and fruitful discussion on the lack of a female protagonist in the four evangelical redactions, I am indebted to her for the great work done together on a collective volume that represents an indispensable exegetical-cultural setting for this essay. The volume in question is *I vangeli. Narrazione e storia*,[17] published in the series La Bibbia e le donne, another great accomplishment for European feminist exegesis.[18]

The scholars mentioned so far, both men and women, will excuse me if, in order not to weigh down the text, I do continually refer to their writings, and in the notes I limit myself to mentioning other references or what seems to me strictly necessary.

In conclusion, I must say that I myself have returned several times to the subject of female discipleship: in addition to my doctoral thesis on the Gospel of Luke,[19] I have dealt with this topic in various essays, from which I can do nothing other than draw some conclusions.[20]

Finally, I cannot forget that, when I was not yet seventeen, a Jesuit priest who was in charge of my formation asked me to study the figure of Mary Magdalene in the four Gospels. Many years later, Professor Magnus Löhrer, then rector of the Pontifical Athenaeum St. Anselmo, asked me to work on the subject of women's discipleship in Luke's Gospel, both for my licentiate thesis and doctoral theses. Since then, I have familiarized myself with a literature then unknown to me, that of feminist critical exegesis. The question of the presence of women in the first Christian tradition continues to be one of the cores of my research.

Finally, to Professor Pius-Ramon Tragan, to his Anselmian lessons, his publications, and the attention with which he followed my doctoral thesis, but also to the inexhaustible discussions with him over the years on the state of biblical studies, I owe everything I know on how to approach the texts of Scripture with passion, rigor, and intellectual honesty.

Chapter 2

More Than Just Preliminaries

Veniamus ad illam, veniamus ad Magdalenam.

Ambrose, *De Isaac et Anima*

A CONSTRUCTED CHARACTER?

Among the many transformations promoted by the Second Vatican Council was the attempt to give back to Mary Magdalene her face and her story—those that, though handed down from the Gospel texts, were forgotten or altered by the subsequent tradition. In the *Dies irae*, a thirteenth-century hymn attributed to Thomas of Celano and formerly part of the Catholic Requiem Mass, we used to sing, *Qui Mariam absolvisti et latronem exaudisti*. The identification of Mary Magdalene with the sinner of the Gospel of Luke had penetrated the theology, worship, and spirituality of the Catholic Church. Since 1969, the text of the sequence has been changed to *Peccatricem qui solvisti et latronem exaudisti*. This is a rather clumsy attempt, perhaps since the hymn was composed in the thirteenth century, and one cannot expect it to reflect modern critical exegesis of the Gospels. But it is also praiseworthy because it affirms the principle that traditions can change, because they reflect ideas and desires, not only of the times in which they originated, but also of those that transmit them. And Vatican II, like it or not, was a time when the critical study of the Bible and Tradition had made available to churches a huge wealth of discoveries, indications, and suggestions.

Perhaps we cannot assume that sooner or later, in Easter morning processions, especially in southern Italy, the statue of Mary, mother of Jesus, will be replaced with that of the disciple of

Magdala, although none of the Gospels speak of an apparition of the Risen Lord to his mother, while all four present the female Galilean disciple at Jesus's tomb on Easter morning. But we can at least aspire to a little influence on the homilies of parish priests who guide the processions.

To pretend to revise the tradition does not mean apologizing for arbitrariness. That the Earth was the center of the universe was an ancient and well-founded belief, just as Mary Magdalene was the forgiven sinner and lover of the Nazarene. It took time for the first, which had to do with the order of the universe, to be refuted. However, the latter, which has to do with the anthropological status and the structure of societies and churches, is still very difficult to do away with. Starting from the third century, the identification of three Gospel figures, who in the texts have each their own distinctive traits, have been conflated: Mary of Magdala, Mary of Bethany, and the forgiven sinful woman. We owe this to a homily of Gregory the Great,[1] which, continually reiterated throughout the Middle Ages, has exerted such a powerful claim on the Christian imagination that it is still difficult to undermine today.

With this identification, what was most characteristic of the Magdalene, that is, that she followed Jesus from Galilee to Golgotha and was the first witness to the resurrection, became secondary, while theological rhetoric turned the Galilean female disciple into an artificial character with a thousand faces. This fact is masterly summarized by Elena Giannarelli:

> Disciple of Jesus, apostle of the apostles, sent by Christ himself to announce His resurrection to others; wealthy believer, repentant sinner, redeemed prostitute; often mistaken for the sister of Martha and Lazarus; author of the fourth gospel; bride or companion of the Lord; Mother of his children and foundress of the Merovingian dynasty; evangelist of Marseille; wife of Saint Paul; adulteress saved from being stoned to death; a prominent figure of the nascent Church in opposition to Peter; even a symbol of Wisdom: these are just some of the identities attributed to the woman of Magdala over the centuries by the New Testament and the Apocrypha, by ecclesiasti-

cal writers and Fathers of the Church, by medieval and ancient exegetes and medieval mystics, by popular legends and novelists of great success and few scruples.[2]

And the list could continue.

A popular tradition, widespread in some areas in Germany, Austria, and northern Italy, according to which the Magdalene is the patroness of winemakers, imagines her as the wife of John the Evangelist, abandoned on her wedding day when her husband became a disciple of Jesus thanks to the miracle of water turned into wine. According to yet another novel built around a manuscript attributable to her, the wedding at Cana would have been her marriage with John the Baptist. However, John was a difficult and violent man, who fortunately would leave her widowed. Thus, she becomes free to marry—at last—Jesus.[3]

Nor should we forget how powerful the contribution of the iconographic tradition has been in this regard. This was clearly displayed at an exhibition held in Florence.[4] In short, the woman of Magdala, of whom we know from the Gospels only that she was a disciple of Jesus, paid the price for the immense fortune that her figure had in the collective imagination throughout the centuries. This idea is rendered by the title of Régis Burnet's book *Marie-Madeleine (Ier–XXIe siècle): de la pécheresse repentie à l'épouse de Jésus* (Mary Magdalene from the first to the twentieth centuries: From repentant sinner to the wife of Jesus).[5]

Therefore, the tradition has insisted on a character functional to the diffusion and preservation of the faith of a Church in which the presence of women has always been at least numerically significant, but where there has been an equally vigorous effort to exclude or circumscribe women's exercise of authority. For this, in the West, the image of the sinner, converted by love and perennially penitent, has prevailed and imposed itself over all the others. It is the image of an Eve finally redeemed thanks to asceticism and penitence, a more realistic ethical model than the inaccessible Mary, the Virgin Mother. Besides, the Eve-Magdalene binomial has ancient roots because it is already present in early Christian writers such as Hippolytus,[6] the fathers of the Greek tradition such as Gregory of

Nyssa, and of the later Latin tradition such as Hilary of Poitiers[7] or Ambrose.[8]

Of course, the Copernican Revolution and the recovery of women's history are two orders of different magnitude. Yet it is of capital importance to free the female disciple of Jesus from all the masks that she has been asked to wear by a tradition that has simultaneously regarded her as an indispensable protagonist of the story of Jesus of Nazareth and also as the object of every form of symbolic appropriation or imaginative reworking.[9] This means that even biblical women are no longer to be considered mere objects of men's thought and fantasies, but to be recognized as specific subjects in the history of faith in Jesus of Nazareth, as historical people and literary characters. What is at stake here is the subtle but decisive anthropological revolution that today comes under the heading of "gender criticism."

The Duty to Recover Historical Memory

Memory narrates, constructs, and destroys, interprets and adulterates, projects, summarizes, and performs, analyzes and synthesizes. And life, as we know well, feeds on memory. Long or short memory, it does not matter: we always act on what we remember, on what has been transmitted to us. Plato theorized it, while we experience it in diverse ways day by day. Faith also feeds on memory, both individual and collective. We always start from what has been transmitted to us, positively or negatively, by addition or subtraction, but always from a heritage of convictions and stereotypes, of acceptances and refusals, of emotions and reflections. Fortunately, in the modern era, transmission of memory has also meant a return to the sources, to the discovery of the root of what we have received, of what we think and believe, to purify our memory from its infinite rewrites.

It may have been a naive and sometimes critical return that has served to demystify how memory is altered and transformed in preservation and transmission. We can no longer do without this return *ad fontes*. This is how memory is preserved from the arbitrary: restart from the beginning, accept it as a rule and benchmark. Thus, historical memory is not arbitrary and tendentious, but acknowledgment of what has been and a respectful attempt to understand it for what it was, as far as possible, without arrogance. This is what I propose to do with Mary of Magdala, the Galilean female disciple of the Nazarene prophet. However, I know well that many will be perplexed by this attempt.

Today it seems that the recovery of historical memory does not deserve widespread attention or large financial investment: the golden age of archival, documentary, archaeological, and philological research is now behind us. The critical investigation of the traces of history, whether imprinted in the subsoil or in books, in spoken or written language, in memories preserved and transmitted, is barely carried out by the passionate effort of a few, and often devalued and ridiculed by many. In our time, characterized by a clear intergenerational gap and by the refusal, even in the scientific field, to give credit to the different forms of historical reconstruction, trying to recapture the historical memory of a Gospel character like Mary of Magdala can be anachronistic or naive, if not useless. Particularly in the context of religious beliefs, all united by the pursuit of emotional experience and without culture, what dominates today is what sociologist Olivier Roy has called "holy ignorance," a clear symptom of a religious revivalism that must be understood as a consequence of globalization and the crisis of cultures.[10]

We see the emergence of new hermeneutical paradigms, between individual narcissism and nostalgia for ancient comprehensive visions.[11] If a philosophy of history that places the stories of individuals into those of peoples within the fresco of a "great story" from the Big Bang to eternity, is now considered illusory, even the effort to recover the traces imprinted in history by specific characters is perceived as a visionary fantasy. Personally, I remain completely convinced that, especially regarding religious knowledge and conviction, one should keep on guard and persevere in historical investigation, even more when dealing with female figures and characters, that is, with the traces of the presence of women in human history, with their contribution of thought and action to the development of the historical, political, and religious events of the humanity. Women have given much more to human history than just the survival of the species. With strength and determination, the patriarchal culture has built the golden legend of the alleged universality of the masculine through the transmission of a mutilated memory, which has pushed women's lives beyond the margin of collective memory and handed it down with stories of subordination.

If today, in any field of knowledge, research on women abandons the historical perspective instead of insisting on a documentary recovery, the risk of condemning women to oblivion is higher than we can imagine. Indeed, historiographical survey has shown that, recurrently and well before any recent feminism, the problem of female marginalization has repeatedly surfaced to consciousness and the need for new social attitudes has been postulated, one capable of rendering justice for the discrimination based on gender difference. In the collective consciousness, however, times of awareness of the history of women have always been followed by long pauses of oblivion that have forced researchers to start over each time. Only historical accuracy can save the achievements of nineteenth- and twentieth-century feminisms from being handed over to new forms of oblivion.

In such a very precise context as that of biblical research, a vein of feminist exegesis in the last decades has taken on with determination the task of giving a face and voice, especially regarding the canonical Gospels, to female protagonists, not only as literary figures but also as historical disciples of Jesus of Nazareth, witnesses of the resurrection, and as apostles engaged in spreading the first Christian proclamation at least as much as the male disciples. Thanks to an investigation of the evangelical texts free from stereotypes acquired through a sequence of distorting mirrors that lasted thousands of years, it became possible to distance from the artificial Magdalene built in the laboratory of tradition. A Magdalene who is not the forgiven prostitute, who does not have blond hair as in Masaccio's painting of the crucifixion, or the tragic features of the eternal penitent like in Donatello's sculpture. A Magdalene who is not, as someone has said, "a synthetic character,"[12] the result of later projections, but is restored to the story of Jesus and his disciples before and after Easter. In this way, she can question the churches as well as say something to men and women today.

16

Of course, now no one thinks that the canonical Gospels tell the story of Jesus of Nazareth "as it actually took place." Not only were the criteria and requisites necessary to compose a historical work at that time far different from those that today distinguish a chronicle from a novel; even the intention that guided each evangelist in the composition of his Gospel is not the one that presides over a work that, especially for us today, we could call "historical": despite their literary form of narration or, as Luke states, his "orderly account" (1:3), the Gospels have captured how much of the story of the Nazarene had deposited in the historical memory of his followers and present him in terms of an announcement of salvation.

Yet there is always a "yet"! Even within individual canonical Gospels are preserved some traditions that can be considered true "relics" of historical documentation. They come mainly from the oral tradition, which the ancients considered a highly reliable source, and sometimes written traditions.

Therefore, as there are archaeological and epigraphic finds, even in the ancient writings there are some literary testimonies of what "really happened." Starting with them, using a process involving cross-competencies, it is possible to arrive at reconstructions that are sometimes appropriate, sometimes risky, always questionable, but still useful because they tell us something different from what we already know, think, and believe based on what has been handed down to us. Thus, recovering the elements of historicity in the Gospels involves cross-competencies, elaborating and evaluating hypotheses, and, finally, choosing the one that, until proven otherwise, appears to be the most plausible.

On the other hand, writing about something always means taking a position and is always a political fact. It was so for the fathers of the Church, and it is the same for us as well. We do not write for ourselves, but for others, to disseminate ideas and convictions; and if today we sometimes change position, it is always based on new elements emerging from an honest and fruitful scientific comparison. By virtue of my training and convinced that I can contribute to a cultural and theological debate on the recovery of female protagonists in the history of Christian origins, I have a responsibility to look at Mary of Magdala in a historical perspective and to seek in the canonical sources as much as they can offer us on a woman whose decisive participation in the original elaboration of the faith in the Risen One and in its first dissemination has been accepted with increasing difficulty. I hope in this way to contribute to what is now indispensable to foster and support within the various Christian churches the transformations necessary to be "inside" and not "outside" our time.

Returning Mary to the Gospels

Of Mary's legend the passages have been clarified, the goals have been identified, and the function, sometimes transgressive and more often repressive, has been unmasked for the history of women. The feminist literature on this subject is vast. And it helped at least to limit the viral effect that the *Golden Legend* of the Dominican Jacopo da Varagine, who was archbishop of Genoa from 1292 to 1298, had on the Christian West.[13] This work has been the keystone of the construction of the Magdalene character, given that writers and painters have drawn exhaustively on its narrative, which is enriched with invented biographical facts and hagiographic rather than historical details.

But regarding the Gospels, we must ask, When the canonical Gospels speak of Mary of Magdala, do they tell us something, albeit a little, of a concrete person, or is it pure literary fiction? But, then again, what function was the literary representation of the Galilean female disciple who witnessed the Easter events meant to have? What function did it have? The problems that the reading and interpretation of the Gospels bring with them concern their historical value and their literary character: To what extent do they preserve traces of a story that deserves to be remembered, albeit with the uncertainties and ambivalences typical of any story, to not relegate Jesus of Nazareth to the sphere of the great religious myths?

We wonder whether Mary, even before being the protagonist of the stories about Jesus narrated by the ancient tradition and the evangelists, has intersected the history of the Nazarene and precisely for that must be remembered by all those who wanted to write and talk about him, or whether the Mary recounted by the evangelists is relegated to a literary function that she carries out in the theological framework of their four narrations to the point of completely undoing her historical reality. In short, is Mary Magdalene merely a literary character with a theological function, or is she the leader of the group of the Galilean female disciples of Jesus of Nazareth, who remained faithful to the end, and precisely for this reason she becomes prominent in the tradition on Jesus to the point that none of the evangelists can do without remembering her?

It is then necessary to clarify what theological-ecclesial function each evangelist attributes to the memory of Mary, the disciple of Jesus. In this regard, a comparison is enlightening and, at the same time, emblematic: if we consider the exegetical history of the so-called Gospel testimony of Jesus's primacy (Matt 16:13–19), what catches our attention is the different theological relevance that Peter and Mary Magdalene acquire in the course of the tradition. The account of Peter's profession of faith in the region of Caesarea Philippi (Matt 16:13–16) begins from a starting point like the one on which the tradition of Mary Magdalene is based: Peter played a role of primary importance within the group of disciples of Jesus as Mary did in the group of female disciples. On this, the overlapping confirmations are many.

In Matthew's Gospel, the information on Peter's leadership role is amplified in scope and meaning: in the process of defining the *auctoritates* on whose foundation the different churches will give strength and legitimacy to the traditions of Jesus and the kerygma of salvation, Matthew 16:13–19 is one of the texts that has most marked the Christian tradition and the life of the churches. It is, however, a fact established by recent exegesis that the promises of Jesus to Peter represent a Matthean amplification of the account of his confession on the road to Caesarea Philippi of Mark 8:27–30. They respond to a Jewish-Christian community in need of vigorous strengthening of identity. In fact, it must overcome the crisis of separation from the synagogue, and it is therefore necessary to base its religious autonomy exclusively on its own past and, above all, on the will and authority of Jesus himself (see also Matt 23:8–11). The evangelist suggests that his community refer to the figure of Peter to find in him the representative par excellence of the first generation of Jesus's disciples, and thus a solid foundation for its identity and for building its own historical memory disengaged from the Jewish authorities.

No one questions that such a Matthean literary and theological construction has a strong historical root in the role played by Peter in the group of Jesus's disciples before and after Easter, nor denies that there is a precise correspondence between person and literary character. If Matthew, two generations removed from the events of Easter and in a delicate and decisive moment in the history of his community like that of the separation from the synagogue, wanted and was able to present Peter as the guarantor of the tie of continuity with Jesus of Nazareth and the stability of the Church born of Jesus's resurrection, it is because the tradition of Peter had already begun to build and impose itself.[14] Other traditions confirm this, for example, Jesus's attribution of the role of strengthening his brothers to Peter (Luke 22:32), the belief of a primitive Easter apparition to Peter (Luke 24:34; see 1 Cor 15:5), and the Risen Lord's triple injunction to Peter during the apparition at the Lake of Tiberias to take upon himself the pastoral responsibility of the community (John 21:15–17). It must also be assumed that, even in this case as in Mathew's Gospel, the tradition has updated historical data in an ecclesial function, in relation, that is, to the new challenges faced by the communities: the problem of historical continuity with the group of disciples of Jesus, for Luke; the risk of splitting apart, for the second ending of the Fourth Gospel.

However, this is not the case for Mary of Magdala, the first witness to the event of Jesus's resurrection. The exegetical history of the Gospel texts that see her as the protagonist follows in fact a nonlinear trajectory that does not proceed by amplification but, rather, by diminution. In this regard, the distance between the Synoptics and John is eloquent and confirms that the reference to her and to the other female disciples takes on a different ecclesiological relevance for the proto-Christian communities that are the background of the Gospel compositions.

Following this first series of observations, others immediately derive from the theological and not just religious character of the Gospel writings. Even before the added value that these writings take as a result of a process of canonization, which confers on them the character of principle and foundation, hence of "rule" of the ecclesial faith, we must recognize that they were neither born nor spread as mere religious literature. Their authors in fact set up a kerygmatic and therefore theological claim: their writings convey a message of salvation according to which faith in Jesus, particularly in his death and resurrection, becomes the foundation and means of eternal salvation.

Evidently, none of the New Testament hagiographers foresaw that his writing would become universal *regula fidei*, but certainly each of them considered his authoritative text in view of the growth in faith of the community/communities to which it was addressed. For this reason, all the different New Testament writings have a character that is, at the same time, descriptive and prescriptive in the conviction of conveying the "what" and the "how" of faith. In this trajectory, which goes from the facts to their transposition in a kerygmatic key to foster conversion and access to salvation, what process of theological representation do those undergo who have been part of the history of the Nazarene? We know very well about Jesus: the prophet of Galilee is recognized and celebrated as the one whom the Father raised from the dead and as the fulfillment of the salvation promised to Israel and awaited by all peoples. But what about the other protagonists of his public life, which goes from his baptism in the Jordan to the events of Easter; what can we say about them? For Peter, the trajectory within the Gospels and the Acts of the Apostles, as we have seen, is easily identifiable. The same, albeit in different terms, can be said for Paul, whose self-witness is imperative, supported also by the account of Acts, and whose epistolary production is also significant. As for most of the others in the group of the Twelve, they are figures who, along the process that confers weight and theological-ecclesial function to the historical data, do not receive great individual relevance; even their traces will be lost in legendary local traditions. It must be surprising, however, that the fate of Mary Magdalene will be only partially similar to theirs, given the quite different relevance this disciple takes in the Gospel accounts of Jesus's death and resurrection and, above all, the apostolic investiture that, according to the Gospel of John, she receives from the Risen One; nothing of the sort is said of Bartholomew, or of Judas Thaddeus, Thomas, or Philip.

Ambivalence, therefore, distinguishes from the early Christian times the construction of the memory around Mary Magdalene: on the one hand, in the tradition of the great Church, the first traces of a downsizing of her figure will result in a progressive annulment of her apostolic role and in an amplification instead of her value as a strong model for penance and conversion. This is already present within the Gospels themselves, following an inverse process to that of Paul and, above all, Peter. On the other hand, in the so-called apocryphal tradition, Mary is exalted for her leadership role, but she is also relegated to the margins and is destined to disappear soon. And this same ambivalence, whereby it is not possible to completely erase her memory, but at the same time it is not possible to fully recognize her role as evangelist and apostle, will also be reflected in the rich flowering of legends that will punctuate the development of her cult and devotion.

However, her figure has never been used in such a way as to allow the churches to develop a structure that does not exclude women from any role of apostolic responsibility. This fact can be seen in both the Eastern Churches, where since antiquity the liturgy commemorates on the second Sunday after Easter the spice bearers that go to the tomb, and, in particular, in the Western tradition, in which from the beginning, the understanding of the title of "apostle of the apostles" is totally distorted and, with it, the theological-ecclesial meaning of the mandate:[15] suffice it to recall here that already Hippolytus, between the second and third centuries, puts the title of "apostola apostolorum" in relation to the overcoming of the sin of Eve,[16] thus giving birth to that superimposition, which will dominate the entire Western tradition, of Mary of Magdala and the great sinner, and precisely the embodiment, like Eve, of female seductiveness. There is more, however: the identity between Eve and Mary of Magdala serves many authors to solve an otherwise insidious question, that is, the reason why the Risen One has manifested himself above all to women. Significantly, then, a theological motivation comes into play: since Eve was the first sinner, it was necessary that a woman be the first to announce salvation. This is an argument that, according to Romanos the Melodist (sixth century), can be a consolation for Peter and the disciple whom Jesus loved to justify the Lord's decision to reveal himself first to a woman![17]

The first step, then, is to put order among the Gospel accounts that mention Mary of Magdala, avoiding unnecessary confusions or overlaps. Described one by one, the female characters become important pieces of the history of a prophet from Galilee, sentenced for his claim to interpret and actualize the definitive coming of the kingdom of God, and whose disciples, after his death, have seen him alive and, for this, have made of his person, his message, and, above all, his death and resurrection the foundation of an announcement of salvation for all.

Very rapidly, these elements become increasingly vague and, regarding Mary of Magdala, what was true for the first apostolic preaching is no longer valid for the churches of the second or third generation. Before examining the texts, it seems important to me to try again to clarify whether the name and, above all, the title with which this woman is mentioned in the Gospels can tell us something about her identity.

A Name, a City

The fact of the matter is we know little about her; but to make things up is useless.

Stefano De Luca, *Magdala Project*

About Mary Magdalene, as with many of the characters who appear in the Gospel narratives, we know very little. The risk of leaving room to the imagination is therefore very high. After all, the exegetical history of the evangelical figures shows that, stronger than the sobriety of the texts, but also of any intellectual rigidity or iconoclastic rigor, it is the anthropological need for verbal elaborations or visual representations that leads to the exuberant and pervasive creation of myths and legends. This is especially true in the Western Christian tradition, which distanced itself from the biblical prohibition of forging images, which was later reconfirmed by the Islamic tradition.

23

The anthropological-cultural tendency to "fill the gaps" is a serious fact because, through the formation of stable family and social traditions, it ensures the survival of human groups. Paradoxically, however, it also fosters their fluidity: precisely because it becomes expression, verbal or visual, tradition is fixed and preserved. However, since the objectivation process is based on changeable subjects and is almost inexhaustible, it can be accordingly transformed and modulated in a way suited to always new cultural horizons and new socioreligious needs.

If we want to remain strictly faithful to the given text, we must recognize that we know a name and, probably, a place of origin for this woman: nothing more. Whether the name is real, since almost all the female characters of the Gospels are called "Mary," we cannot say. Undoubtedly, however, this name and the designation ἡ Μαγδαληνή represent a stable literary fact: in all four Gospels, this is how the Galilean female disciple is mentioned. What is being transmitted to us by this literary evidence?

A Name

Mary Magdalene is explicitly mentioned twelve times in the canonical Gospels,[18] and always in the same grammatical form: a name accompanied by an appellation, in turn preceded by the definite article (ἡ Μαγδαληνή = the Magdalene). Only once does Luke explicitly say that it is a nickname (8:2: ἡ καλουμένη Μαγδαληνή = called Magdalene). Although she is named much less than Peter (ninety-four times!), Mary is still one of the most mentioned characters. And among women, if we exclude Mary, the mother of Jesus (eighteen times), she is certainly the most mentioned. This is not without problems, though.

Mary of Magdala appears, in fact, only in the passion narratives, and her memory therefore goes back to the most ancient historical tradition of the Nazarene, the one that, from the very beginning and after the facts, had translated the memory of the tragic Easter events into an announcement of salvation. Except in Luke, who, as we shall see, anticipates the mention of the female disciple by inserting her already in the presentation of the mission of Jesus in Galilee (8:2), Mary and the other women are therefore essential characters on the scene of Jesus's passion, to the point that it is impossible to tell it and announce its salvific value without talking about her and the other women. Among those of the various women, her name is the only one that is consistent. No one can therefore doubt that this woman was well known as Mary Magdalene and that this name evoked an authoritative character: without her we cannot speak of the cross and resurrection.

This, however, exacerbates even more the problem of her total absence from the rest of the Gospel narratives. Except for a Lucan quote, Mary and the other women completely disappear from the account of Jesus's missionary itinerancy. It is not by chance that the ancient fathers, unable to understand such inconsistent incongruity, have clustered in her figure all the women, anonymous or not, who play a part in the story of Jesus before Easter: the sinner of Luke 7:36–50, and the anonymous woman who anoints the head of Jesus at the beginning of his passion (Mark 14:1–9 par.); for John, she is Mary, the sister of Marta and Lazarus instead (12:1–8). For those who want to stick to the literary evidence, it is best to try to explain the incongruity than to mystify it, even if any attempt at an explanation remains entirely hypothetical.

If we read the Gospels from the beginning, the absence of women from the story of Jesus is surprising: the ones called are only men; the Twelve are all men; the disciples seem, at least at first sight, only men. I will discuss this further later. For now, suffice it to say that even if the Gospels are read from the beginning, the arrival on the scene of Mary of Magdala and of others in the stories of the passion is truly unexpected, to say nothing of the powerful way it is described. It is a completely unprecedented matter: how to explain it?

But the question should, at least in part, be reversed: it is a matter of explaining why Mary leaves the scene, and not because she enters it. In fact, according to the history of their composition, but also based on their internal theological rationale, the Gospels are to be read from the end, not from the beginning. The history of the early Christian preaching begins with the announcement of the resurrection, and by virtue of that, the whole story of the Nazarene who has prophesied the coming of the kingdom of God is then understood and told as ἐυαγγέλιον (gospel, good news): this is the term by which the earliest of the Gospels, Mark, introduces his narration, declaring its character and purpose (1:1–15).

On this basis, then, the absence of Mary from the Gospel accounts that precede the passion could be well explained in ideological terms: a few decades after Jesus's life, the memory of this woman had acquired weight and authority in environments considered marginal with respect to the constitution of what will be called the "Great Church." Therefore, we cannot be surprised by an operation that has, if not completely eradicated, at least reduced the role of the female figures in the story of Jesus.

Besides, between the first and second generations of Christians, women had been prominent in the first community of disciples and had taken part in the elaboration and dissemination of the proclamation,[19] but were subsequently and gradually removed from apostolic roles. The silence over them could therefore be one of the signs of this process of marginalization already recognizable in the canonical Gospels. There is certainly something very true in all of this, but to avoid suggesting an indiscriminate misogynist fury that altered the traits of primitive preaching of Jesus, a further clarification must be made, at least for the three Synoptic Gospels.

From a careful reading of the first three canonical Gospels, clearly their authors addressed an audience including several women. They took part in the life of the disciples of Jesus since the very beginning. They witnessed the preaching of Jesus, which, having never lost its popular connotation, has always been addressed to all. As proof of this, it is sufficient to consider that female figures are the protagonists of several parables (Matt 13:33, and Luke 13:20–21, the parable of the yeast; Luke 15:8–10, the parable of the lost coin; Luke 18:1–8, the parable of the widow and the unjust judge), have exemplary function (Mark 12:41–44 resumed by Luke 21:1–4, the widow's offering; Luke 7:36–50, a sinful woman forgiven; Mark 14:3–9, the anointing at Bethany), or they are the protagonists of miracle stories (Mark 1:29–31, Simon's mother-in-law; Mark 5:25, a woman healed, Mark 7:25–30, the Syrophoenician woman's faith; Luke 7:11–17, Jesus raises the widow's son at Nain). Worth noting, however, is that these women are always anonymous figures. Also, it should not be forgotten that regarding women, there has always been a kind of "implicit fascination," given that languages, both ancient and modern, assume that masculine grammatical form has an inclusive function. It is therefore plausible that every time that the "disciples" are mentioned, it may be referring to both men and women. If it is therefore true that the canonical Gospels allow a glimpse in the background communities of men and women who believe in the Risen One, it is also true that when they refer to community roles and functions, the impression is that women should instead disappear completely from the horizon. This is the case for the calling stories, for example, which we will examine later. It seems to me that we cannot add more on this topic.

It should be noted, however, that if the name of Mary Magdalene is so firmly affirmed in the stories of the passion, it was obviously impossible to present it in any other way: some of the disciples had to ensure continuity between the before and after of Easter, between the death and resurrection, and everyone knew that it was her. But, as we shall see, both Matthew and, above all, Luke will do all they can to mitigate the scope of her presence, and in their passion narratives, Mary's role of disciple and leader of the group of the Galilean female disciples will start to lose importance.

One final observation regarding the appellation that accompanies Mary's name: The nickname "Magdalene" is one of the twenty-eight toponyms that recur, in six different grammatical forms, in the four canonical Gospels. Scholars believe that the omission of the article in the appellation should be considered the most widespread form in both the classical and the New Testament Greek and, conversely, that the construction with the article is a sign of a specific intention. Besides the twelve times when it refers to Mary the Magdalene, the article is used seven times for Jesus, who is qualified as "the Nazarene."[20] Based on these considerations, Thompson is quite right when she concludes, "The frequency and consistency with which the form is used signifies widespread and accepted usage. The prominence of the form also indicates that the basic narratives of crucifixion, burial, and resurrection contained a personal name, in a specific formulation, which could not be minimalized nor omitted."[21] Finally, is it because she was a free woman, that is, she was not married or was a widow, that her name is not accompanied by that of her father, husband, or her son? It is quite plausible, in short, that the nickname "the Magdalene" is due to the place of origin of Mary, that is, from the city of Magdala.

An exception must be mentioned here, however, since it keeps alive another interpretive vein already present in the patristic and medieval tradition. Based on the philological analysis, Maria Luisa Rigato proposes that the passive participle of the Hebrew verb *gadal*, whose meaning would be "the one who was made great, the Magnified,"[22] is at the basis of the Greek expression ἡ Μαγδαληνή.

This is not a completely new line of inquiry, because two authoritative ancient fathers, Origen and Jerome, had already mixed together toponymy and philology. The former, who follows Matthew's account (27:55–56) and pursues a singular updating of the text of Isaiah 27:11, intending it as an appeal to women to abandon Judaism and turn instead to the New Testament, pays particular attention to Mary and believes that her name comes from the name of her homeland, a place that means *magnificatio*, to make great.[23] For his part, Jerome, starting from the Hebrew meaning of the word *Magdala*, that is, "tower of God," describes it as the "turreted one," the "guardian of the tower," because, unlike the apostles who have long doubted, the Magdalene was immediately certain of having encountered the Risen One.[24] The same line extends to the Middle Ages, and for Jacopo da Varagine and his *Golden Legend*, some of the possible meanings of the term *Magdalene* are *fortificata*, *invicta*, or even *magnifica* ("fortified," "invincible," "magnificent," respectively). Although these are certainly fascinating suggestions, the toponymic value of *Magdalene* remains completely credible. For this reason, though it may tell us very little about Mary, we must keep in mind what, today, can be said about the city that is supposed to have been her place of origin.

A City

Thanks to the Magdala Center project, the Legionaries of Christ, and the excavations directed by Dina Avshalom-Gorni and Arfan Najar, of the Israel Antiquities Authority, some residential quarters and an interesting synagogue building with various furnishings have been discovered, all dating back to the first century.[25] Thanks also to the archaeological excavations of the Magdala Project, which had been carried out for several years in a nearby site, and to which the Custody of the Holy Land has recently given new planning, today we know many things about this city located on the northwest coast of Lake Tiberias. Perhaps, however, they can help us only in part to better identify the historical features of Mary Magdalene. Hopefully, they can at least serve as a brake for new tourist-religious claims that, at a time when all have by now appropriated, even inappropriately, the cause of women, could give new impetus to devotions to Mary Magdalene based on ancient legends that have little to do with the Gospel witness.

The project, sponsored by the Studium Biblicum Franciscanum of Jerusalem, will in the future be made available to the public by the Pilgrimage Office of the Diocese of Vicenza, under an agreement with the Custody of the Holy Land.[26] Directed by Father Stefano De Luca, the Magdala Project resumed the excavations begun in the 1950s by Father Virgilio Corbo based on information that archaeologists Sylvester Saller and Bellarmino Bagatti had collected firsthand from the last inhabitants of the site in 1935 before it was totally destroyed by Israeli bulldozers in 1948. The findings of the excavations—a convent and, in all probability, even a church—have confirmed an extensive list of literary testimonies that, over a period of centuries ranging from 1 BC to the seventeenth century AD, inform us of a constant interest in a site that has always been revered, in the Christian era, as the place where "Mary was born."[27] The name has a Semitic origin, *Migdal nunaja*[28] (the tower of fish), or Greek, *Tarichea* (Salty Fish). And because of its quality as an administrative center of southwestern Galilee and the main fish market in the area, it represented, before the construction of Tiberias, the largest city on the lake, a vital hub on the Via Maris, which went from Damascus to Egypt,[29] that is, to the sea, and made Galilee an important crossroads.

It is possible that in the days of Jesus the inhabitants of Magdala were about forty thousand. Its flourishing economy, attested by the large amount of coins found, could also count on naval carpentry and the craftsmanship of dyeing and silk weaving. The historical events of the era of Roman domination have given this city Hellenistic-Roman cultural traits. The great excavation work of the last decades has brought to light an imposing urban fabric, rich in public and private buildings. An elegant mosaic found in one of the rooms of the Thermae brings us, with its symbols, to the daily life of this city built on work, that is, fishing, agriculture, and commerce, and leisure, that is, gyms and spas.

From the Gospel texts it does not appear that Jesus ever went to Magdala, even if some authors wanted to see a reference to the immediate surroundings of this city in the mention of the "Magadan region" in Matthew 15:39 and Dalmanuta in Mark 8:10, that is, the place of the feeding of the four thousand.

Although it is very important for the reconstruction of the cultural and religious situation of Galilee at the time of Jesus, all of this tells us little about Mary. Since Capernaum is in the district of Magdala, one can simply say that Mary comes from the same area of Peter, Andrew, and Philip. Everything else remains precluded to us: whose daughter she was, and what the social level of her family was; if she was religious, married, wealthy; if she followed Jesus because she had heard him preaching in Capernaum or, as evidenced by a tradition taken from Luke (8:2), because she had been healed of a severe form of psychic illness. To imagine her engaged in fishing or at spas, the wife of a trader or a figure on the margins of the social fabric is a pure exercise of the imagination.

Nothing then allows us to substantiate the assumptions that, from the false belief that she was the public sinner mentioned in Luke's Gospel (7:36–50), make her a fallen woman. Like it or not, the Gospels report only what the authors considered important in view of the credibility of the proclamation of faith, and all this, of course, is not.

Does this necessarily mean, as Dauzat suggests, that the attempt to bring the literary testimonies of the Gospels, if and when possible, to the reality of the facts is nothing but a historicist illusion condemned to be thwarted by one naiveté after another?[30] Precisely because I am convinced of the opposite, I believe that the literary testimony contained in the canonical Gospels can tell us something very important about a female disciple of Jesus who, despite being at the origin of an apostolic genealogy, was condemned to be an apostle without a story.

Chapter 3

Witness to the
Death and Burial

THE FORGOTTEN DISCIPLE:
THE SYNOPTIC GOSPELS

See how the inferior sex of women appears here manlier,
and so everything is reversed.

John Chrysostom, *In Johannem* 82

To define Mary of Magdala from the point of view of her historical
reality first requires us to order the various Gospel narratives that
present the woman of Magdala in terms that sometimes coincide
but diverge at others. The three Synoptics, though they are not
without differences, always portray her together with other women
and as the leader of a small group of female Galilean disciples.
However, in John the historical features of Mary's participation in
the events of the passion fade away and what dominates instead is a
narrative figure with high theological value. In the Fourth Gospel,
Mary is recognized not only as having a preeminent role regarding
the group of women but among the whole community of disciples.

In short, not unlike the ancient fathers, we are also faced with
having to reckon with traditions that differ, if not conflict. But we
approach it differently. The fathers proceeded by systematic logic,
and therefore, at all costs, pursued *concordanctia oppositorum.*
Instead, we moderns, putting aside apologetic anxieties, do not
fear to venture into analytical procedures respectful of diversity,
both morphological and, at times, even at the content level, of the
different traditions.

Even more important, however, is that, unlike the fathers and
their later interpreters, women exegetes have no hesitation in

31

unmasking the role that the *impedimentum sexus* played in the early Christian process of building authoritative figures (*auctoritates*) on whose foundation the development of tradition is upheld and legitimized. The *impedimentum sexus* did not, as is often believed, concern only worship, but it acted as a determining criterion for the exclusion of women from all kinds of ecclesial roles. The foundation of every form of patriarchy, its theological-speculative root, already in biblical times, lies in a gender reading of the myth of the original fall that penalizes women, in an anthropological androcentric vision, and in a monosexist socioreligious order. As far as it concerns us, then, it should not be surprising if we keep in mind the burden that *impedimentum sexus* has represented for the development of the Gospel tradition on Mary of Magdala.

First, we will pay attention to the references to Mary Magdalene, two in the Synoptics and one in John, regarding her presence at the crucifixion and burial. In fact, the substantial difference, internal to the only passion account, between the narration of clear historical events, such as the crucifixion and burial, and stories of apparitions must be respected. In fact, in both, the relationship between history and stories is radically different.

Doubtless for the evangelists, all four Easter events, death-burial and resurrection-apparition, have a kerygmatic character. One is not salvific without the others: here is the strength of the announcement, whether transmitted through a formula of faith or through an entire kerygmatic narration. However, this cannot subtract some events from the history of events and place others in the testimonial history of an individual and collective experience of faith. Both authors and recipients were certainly aware of the substantial difference between stories of events that can also be verified from the outside and stories of experiences pertaining exclusively to the different areas of the practice of faith. Let us therefore consider, first, the Synoptic Gospels. In all three, the explicit mention of Mary of Magdala occurs only in the story of the passion (only Luke mentions her once earlier), and this suggests that this information is present in the earliest stage of the tradition: there is no doubt that immediately after the death and resurrection of the Galilean it was precisely the story of his passion that contributed to the spreading of the memory of the Easter events as an announcement of salvation.

The examination of the earliest of the Gospels, Mark, in which the passion narrative is most likely the primitive nucleus from which the evangelist then composed the rest of his Gospel narration, guarantees a good starting point for a general overview of the three Synoptics. In fact, both Matthew and Luke will draw on Mark's account, if not on a primitive pre-Marcan tradition.

Disciple in Her Own Right: The Gospel of Mark

> There were also women looking on from a distance; among them were Mary Magdalene, and Mary the mother of James the younger and of Joses, and Salome. These used to follow him and provided for him when he was in Galilee; and there were many other women who had come up with him to Jerusalem.
>
> Mark 15:40–41

In Mark, few characters are called by name more than once. Mary of Magdala is named three times, all in the passion narrative: under the cross (15:40), at the burial site (15:47), and at the empty tomb on Easter morning (16:1). In addition, in the so-called second ending of Mark (16:9–20), which scholars believe to be a later addition after the authentic ending of the Gospel (vv. 1–8), her name recurs and is accompanied by some specifications: she is the one from whom, as in Luke (8:2), seven demons had come out, and it is she, as in John (20:11ff.), who is to be the first to see the Risen Lord, but as in Luke (24:10), the disciples do not believe her testimony. These are signs that the passage that today closes the Gospel was written later and has thus been able to incorporate other traditions that had become widespread. In all these three (or four) times, the wording is always Mary the Magdalene (Μαρία ἡ Μαγδαληνή). What was possible to say about this name and its quality as a toponym has been mentioned earlier. Here we are interested rather in the connotation that this character receives within the first of the Gospels in relation to the other protagonists, particularly the other women: What does Mark tell us about her? Did he consider Mary and the other women as part of the group of Jesus's disciples?

The Galilean Female Disciples under the Cross

Let us first begin with how much is explicitly said of this Galilean woman. As we have already mentioned, her name recurs in the passion story three times. This recurrence can be assessed from a double point of view, that of its historical plausibility and that of the meaning that the evangelist attributes to it within the theological order of the whole story.

It is now an accepted fact that the explicit mention of some characters, and especially the nominal lists, show a high rate of historical plausibility. The ancient tradition attributed, in fact, to the reference to known characters, still alive or recently dead, a wide range of credibility. Valid for the lists of the Twelve present in the three Synoptic Gospels and in Acts,[1] or even for that of the three disciples to whom Jesus reserves particular revelations,[2] the criterion must also be valid for the lists of the Galilean women: they attest to the verifiability of an ancient tradition that can be related to precise known people, probably still alive at the time of the formation of the primitive Jesus tradition.

They also attest to some extent to the acquired official stamp, unlike the references to isolated names, which, when they are not just literary constructions, can be considered mostly as traces of local traditions. Both have then quickly merged into more extensive traditional units, such as, for example, the whole narrative of the passion; these units, together with the collections of miracle stories and the parables, or those words and teachings of Jesus that remained etched in the memory of his disciples, became the foundation for the composition of each Gospel. It is therefore evident that the account of Jesus's death and burial bases its historical plausibility on the nominal mention of the three Galilean women: their eyewitness testimony guarantees that Jesus was truly crucified, that he was truly buried, and his tomb was empty the morning after the Sabbath.

In Mark, however, the triple reference presents some differences: at the crucifixion (15:40), the names mentioned are those of Mary of Magdala, Mary the mother of James the younger and Joses,[3] and Salome; while at the burial, only those of Mary of Magdala and Mary the mother of Joses (15:47); and at the empty tomb (16:1), those of Mary of Magdala, Mary the mother of James, and Salome. This can only be explained by hypothesizing the confluence of a plurality of different traditions, which does not weaken, but strengthens its historical value.

The same happens for the lists of the Twelve, which, though more consistent, still present some variants: their transmission inevitably suffers from some uncertainty that is not always possible to account for. It should be noted, however, that, as in the lists of the Twelve, an undisputable priority reserved for Peter is considered the sign of his preeminent role within the group; so we must also consider that Mary, whose name, always used first, here as in the other Synoptics, is evidently presented as the *leader* of the women's group.

Most important, however, is the description that the evangelist offers of the three women called by name among the many present at the crucifixion. It is said that, since Jesus was in Galilee, they "used to follow him and provided for him." In Mark, the use of the verb "to follow" (ἀκολουθέω) is frequent, and he also uses it in the generic sense, as, for example, in the case of the crowd (see 3:7, or 5:24). Only when the women are referenced, however, is the verb "to serve" (διακονέω) connected to the verb "to follow." There is no doubt that, very early on, the Christian tradition must have attributed to the combination *follow-serve* a connotation of discipleship, in continuity with the Jewish practice of discipleship regarding the rabbis.

Thus, a crucial question begins to emerge. Here, the three Galilean women are described starting from the two identifying activities of the disciple, to follow-serve. But we know very well that in all the New Testament writings, the term *disciple* never appears, except once in the case of a woman of Joppa who led a community of widows and who had been resurrected by Peter (Acts 9:36: μαθήτρια). How to assess the gap between reality data and linguistic formalization?

All the languages that have developed within patriarchal cultures, including Greek, assume that the masculine grammatical form also includes the feminine; can we legitimately assume then that when *disciples* appears in the Gospel texts (μαθηταί), the term refers equally to men and women? Isn't it the same when referring generically to sick and possessed persons always using the masculine form (e.g., Mark 1:32)? It will be necessary to return to this point, which is of paramount importance, to clarify the role played by Mary of Magdala among Jesus's followers and within the disciple movement born from the resurrection. For Mark, therefore, three precise women have been following Jesus and have already provided for him since his mission in Galilee.[4] This means that he recognizes them as disciples from the beginning. Moreover, the use of the verbal form of the imperfect (ἠκολούθον καὶ διηκόνουν = "used to follow and provided for him"), indicating prolonged action over time, and the insistence on the strictly personal relationship of these three women with Jesus and his Galilean mission lead us to conclude that the tradition has preserved a testimony about a group of female Galilean disciples of Jesus of which Mary of Magdala was recognized as leader.

There is nothing in this description that allows us to indulge on the *topos* of the penitent sinner, that of the secret lover of Jesus or, even less, on her anti-Eve role.

Not unlike Peter, who leads the group of the Twelve, Mary leads the group of the female disciples of Jesus. But with a significant difference, however: the *leadership* of the group of the Twelve involves, as we shall see, a very strong symbolic meaning; it will easily lend itself to transposition from the prophetic-eschatological level to the juridical-institutional one. The *leadership* of the female group of disciples, despite its historical roots and the strong theological value of their presence in the Easter events, will not find any confirmation in the institutional configuration of the churches.

Two more important observations. The three women mentioned by name are part of a larger group of women "looking on from a distance," and with them, there are also "many other women who had come up with him to Jerusalem." The real possibility that Roman soldiers would allow someone to witness a crucifixion explains the necessity of the adverbial clarification ἀπὸ μακρόθεν (from a distance).

We are interested in highlighting the historical character of the material: the three women confirm the existence of a much larger group of female disciples who cannot therefore be reduced to three. It is hard to say whether this refers to Jesus's mission or reflects the reality of post-Easter communities. However, that the characteristic of this vast group is that of being "disciples" is made clear by the expression "had come up with him to Jerusalem," clearly referring to the need for each one to take up one's own cross (8:34–38) that Jesus imparts just as he, together with his disciples, begins to go up to Jerusalem. However, should the term *discipleship* be intended in a generic sense, or, instead, in a more specific one?

In fact, Jesus addresses this injunction to take up one's cross and to follow him to a group composed of both the crowd and his disciples. Jesus walks in front, and a group of disciples follows him, afraid and dismayed; only to the Twelve, however, does he reserve clear words that tell them what is going to happen in the holy city. When two of the Twelve, the sons of Zebedee, show that they have completely misunderstood the discourse of following and taking up one's cross, this allows him to offer a group lesson on the relationship between the cross and service. As their presence on Golgotha would suggest, can we assume that the female Galilean disciples are also part of this group to whom Jesus closely predicts what will happen in Jerusalem and to whom, more importantly, the Teacher explains the meaning of following and taking up one's cross as a service? Are they also part of the group of the Twelve? We will return shortly to this point. One thing seems certain: a large group of women followed Jesus on the journey that led him to the cross.

At this point, a question arises: If Mark preserves and transmits in the passion narrative a fact as important as the discipleship of the Galilean women, how then can we evaluate his silence on them throughout the previous narrative? Four groups of people come into play: the crowd, the disciples, the Twelve as a whole, and mentions of the Twelve individually or in small groups. But there are also some female characters on whom Jesus exercises his miraculous power, and who are always connected to a particular teaching: Peter's mother-in-law, on whom Jesus works his first miracle of healing and who, once healed, exercises *diaconia* for him (1:29ff.); Jairus, one of the leaders of the synagogue, and his daughter, both protagonists of Mark's only resurrection story (5:21–24; 35–43); the woman suffering from a hemorrhage, whose attitude induces Jesus to overcome one of the fundamental taboos of Judaism, that of women's blood, and prompts a particularly incisive word on the relationship between faith and miracles (5:25–34); the Syrophoenician woman, who, in addition to her daughter's healing, brings Jesus's mission beyond the borders of Israel and brings salvation even to the pagans (8:24–37); and the poor widow's temple offering, which Jesus uses as an example for a teaching on the religious hypocrisy of the rich (13:41–44). At this point, a detailed analysis of each passage would be necessary to postulate the degree of historicity, but it is evident that, given the figures proposed as models, both Jesus's preaching and Mark's Gospel were addressed to an audience that included women.

A second, more pressing question relates not just to the first Gospel but also calls into question all the others: What about the fact that in all the Gospel narratives there is not even one story of calling women to leadership roles?

At the beginning of his Gospel, Mark, immediately after the messianic investiture of Jesus through the baptism and temptations and after the solemn declaration that introduces his kerygmatic mission (1:1–15), adds as the first act of this same mission the story of the call of two pairs of brothers, first Simon and Andrew, and later the two sons of Zebedee, James and John. As its chronological position in the narration suggests, it could be a proleptic explication that is a prelude to the constitution of the group of the Twelve, and clarifies its meaning by attesting that Jesus wanted from the beginning to share his itinerant mission with his disciples and anticipates its subsequent ecclesial reach with the reference to becoming "fishers for people" (1:16–20).

We will return to this text soon. What interests us is this: How can we evaluate the discipleship of the three Galilean women and that of Mary of Magdala, which Mark recounts clearly and precisely in the passion narrative? Is there a decisive value to the fact that in all four Gospels we find no call of Jesus addressed directly to one or more women, as to, for example, Peter and Andrew, James and John, or even Philip and Nathanael?

It is necessary to consider this question. It is too hasty to assert that without a call there is no discipleship, and that since they do not appear to have been called, women are not disciples. It ignores a text of primary importance, from both a historical and theological point of view, like Mark's passion story. It then identifies the two realities, that of the disciples and that of the Twelve, reducing one to the other, thus not even correctly giving a reason for the theological meaning that Mark gives both to Jesus's discipleship and to the post-Easter discipleship.

The Crowd, the Disciples, the Twelve—And the Women?

The Evangelist Mark develops, along the course of his narration, an interesting vision of discipleship.[5] Although implicit, it can be grasped thanks to a succession of tensions, clarifications, and even negations. For Mark, Jesus's discipleship entails, first, a process of distinction: some become recipients of the Teacher's instructions, which are precluded to the crowd. Although they live the experience of inadequacy, which gives rise to resistance and rejection (8:31ff.; 9:31; 10:13), betrayal (14:43ff., 66ff.) and fear (16:8), the disciples are individuals whom Jesus calls around him, confides his intentions, instructs them, and sends them on a mission: between him and the crowd, which remains always the first recipient of his proclamation of the kingdom, we find a group of disciples that ensures that this announcement is not dispersed.

Both the crowd and the group of disciples were present in the life of the prophet of Nazareth. Beyond some rhetorical emphases, insisting on the proportions of the people who attended his preaching (1:45; 2:2; 3:7; 4:1), the fact that Jesus addressed the crowd and had influence over it is confirmed by the decision of the leaders of the Jews to put him to death, just for fear of losing the grip on the people. Because of the crowd, they are always forced to look for a favorable time to do so (14:1–2).

For our question, the distinction between the crowd and the disciples is important. At some point in his ministry, Jesus decided to be accompanied by some disciples and to share with them his missionary journeys, reserving for himself the charismatic role of Teacher. In Mark, this becomes clear precisely from the contrast between the crowd and the disciples (or the Twelve), which contributes greater drama to the story. The "crowd" is the undisputed protagonist of the first part of Jesus's mission: they come to him from everywhere (1:45); they bring him many sick and possessed

(1:32ff.); many people gather around him (2:2) to hear his teaching (2:13b). However, when a huge crowd is gathered around him and Jesus addresses to them the parables of the kingdom (4:1), the process of differentiation begins. Having dismissed the crowd, Jesus explains the meaning of the parables only to the disciples (4:36). It is precisely starting from here and until the entrance in Jerusalem that the narration begins to move on a double level, that of the crowd and that of the disciples.

Moreover, Jesus formalizes this distance because he decides to confer on the group of disciples the status of messianic people. This is the meaning of the Twelve's call "to be with him, and to be sent out to proclaim the message" (3:14): Jesus understands that the gathering of Israel for which he was sent passes from there. In addition, within the group of the women present at the crucifixion, a double level is recognizable as well: there are many women who have followed Jesus in his journey, but there is also the small group of the three Galilean disciples led by Mary of Magdala. The others will leave the scene while the three of them will be mentioned again at the burial site and on the morning of Easter (15:47 and 16:1): they are the witnesses of the events that will become the content of the Christian proclamation—crucifixion, burial, resurrection, and apparitions (see 1 Cor 15:3–5). Is it too far-fetched to believe that the female Galilean disciples had been part of the group of the Twelve? The answer is not easy.

It is now an established fact among scholars that the value of the word *Twelve* is not numeric, but symbolic, that is, it is not reductive but extensive. In fact, it refers to the original Israel, which was constituted of twelve tribes, of which the twelve patriarchs, as collective personalities, were the representative figures. Precisely because of its evocative value, the term *Twelve* refers to an entire people, not to a closed group of twelve men. That the names of the Twelve, whose call establishes the decisive passage of Jesus's mission from popular preaching to the establishment of the new messianic-eschatological Israel, are those of twelve men is therefore quite understandable: such were in fact the ancient founders of the twelve tribes of Israel.

One cannot certainly doubt, however, that women were among the tribes of ancient Israel, so it cannot be doubted that Jesus called them to be part of the new Israel. If, therefore, it was inconceivable that the names of women should appear among the names of the Twelve, it is equally unthinkable to assume that the mention of the "disciples" or the "Twelve" was not meant to refer to a group of Jesus's followers, both men and women. In this case, even the presence of the "Twelve" (Mark 14:17–18) at the Last Supper should be understood in symbolic terms and would therefore not exclude women. If this were at least plausible, perhaps we could finally give up the refrain that the male disciples abandoned Jesus at the time of his arrest, while the women were present under the cross. It is obvious that the passion narrative, especially in its most archaic version, is the result of different, juxtaposed, sometimes contradictory traditions. Forcing it into a narrative continuity that is not its own forces its meanings. It is quite possible then that the disciples who, full of fear, abandon Jesus in the Garden of Gethsemane were *all* the disciples (14:50: ἔφυγον πάντες), without distinction of sex, because the Teacher's destiny is to go to the cross alone. This does not exclude that, as conveyed by an ancient tradition, the female Galilean disciples were present at the crucifixion.

It should also be noted that, at the beginning of Acts, when because of the defection of Judas, it becomes necessary to choose someone to reintegrate the Twelve, Peter specifies that it must be a man (1:21). We cannot indulge in illusions, but we can assume that it was not something that was completely obvious before then if, after Easter, it is necessary to specify it. Conversely, because of the impetus given by Gerd Theissen,[6] sociohistorical studies have debunked the idea that in the first-century Palestine it was impossible for women to participate in groups that practiced a form of itinerant life.

That male and female disciples followed Jesus, listened to his proclamation and teachings, witnessed his miracles, and took part in his mission still tells us nothing, however, about the internal organization of the group. This remains a question difficult to solve. The fact that the tradition conveyed by Mark has listed three men, Peter, John, and James (5:37; 9:2; 13:3; 14:33), and three women, Mary of Magdala, Mary the mother of James the younger and Joses, and Salome (15:40), suggests that the large group of disciples had some distinctions within it, including gender. This is a fact entirely plausible in the Jewish context.

The question of the call stories must then be placed in this context. In Mark, apart from that of the Twelve, as symbol of Jesus's will to establish the new Israel, there is only the call of the two pairs of brothers, Simon and Andrew, and the two sons of Zebedee (1:16–20); from the editorial point of view, it is the first act Jesus performs at the beginning of his mission. The name recurrences and the fact that, apart from Andrew, the other three whom were called intervene several times in Mark's narrative are evidence of the archaic nature of the tradition underlying the story. And, not by chance, the four names are among those of the Twelve.

We can legitimately ask whether, by placing it as a preliminary gesture for the fulfillment of Jesus's mission, Mark does not intend to legitimize from the start the authoritative role of some in the community, ascribing to Jesus himself the will to explicitly call some of them. Such a supposition is reinforced by the expression "I will make you fishers of people," which gives the story a clear ecclesial connotation. If, therefore, the account of the call of the four disciples is to be considered as a paradigmatic representation with an ecclesial function, the absence of female characters is less astonishing. The final redaction of the Gospel occurs at a time when the apostolic role of women in the communities had already been greatly reduced compared to the early times and, with it, their authority. Progressively, women will increasingly become more the caught and less the catchers.

More important, however, seems to me to be another observation and, stemming from it, another question. The observation concerns Mark 15:41—we must consider that if Jesus's discipleship was not based on a claim made by the disciples, but on a free call from the Teacher, these Galilean women are at his crucifixion because they have been called by him to follow in his mission and have served him by participating with him in the announcement of the kingdom. The real question underlying Jesus's discipleship is then this: Why have some men and women been willing to follow a prophet like Jesus? It has already been pointed out how much the socioeconomic situation of Palestine and Galilee at the beginning of the first century was problematic and how this could be considered a strong influence, even if implicit, to feel attracted by Jesus's preaching and touched by his announcement as by a real call.[7]

However, I believe, in this regard, that we should limit ourselves to consider only the importance of economic and social factors, but we must also reflect on the religious anxiety that was present in some sections of the Palestinian population and the extent to which it may have represented the implicit presupposition to recognize in the eschatological message of Jesus not only a generic appeal of the advent of the kingdom, but also a real call to take part in the spread of the kingdom he announced.

This does not conflict in any way with the editorial composition of the various stories of calls and their insistence on the fact that the initiative of the call is always taken, with sovereign will, by Jesus himself: none of those who followed him could claim having done it on their own initiative, but this does not mean we misunderstand the importance of their religious expectations as well. We will return to this point more in detail in the third part of this study. Suffice it to say here that it is very likely that the Galilean women became disciples of Jesus because they felt that his person and his message responded to their messianic expectations.

In conclusion, according to the narrative development in Mark, fairly early enough Jesus clearly perceives the gap between the "crowd" and the "disciples," that is, between the people, at the beginning the only recipients of the announcement of the kingdom, who rush to his preaching and hopes in his healing; and the disciples, men and women who instead agree to embody the content, spirit, and style of his preaching of the kingdom of God (4:11). Jesus does not avoid the crowd (5:14, 24; 6:33; 7:14ff.); twice he feeds them with a multiplication of loaves (6:34ff.; 8:1ff.) and holds back from no one the gifts of his miraculous powers (6:54) and his teaching (7:14; 8:34; 10:1ff.). At the same time, he begins to devote himself more directly to a group of disciples: the evangelist explicitly states that the ones following him are his disciples (6:1); that Jesus sends the Twelve on a mission (6:7ff.) and wants to remain alone with those he sends (6:31) and with his disciples (6:45); and that what determines the distance between the crowd and the group of disciples is the christological confession (8:27ff.). Even if the crowd does not disappear from the scene, the disciples are not confused with it (8:34ff.; 9:14ff.; 10:46). Only to the disciples are reserved the first two predictions of the passion (8:31; 9:30ff.), while to the Twelve Jesus imparts the instruction on humility (9:33) and the third prediction of the passion (10:33).

For Mark, these disciples are the nucleus around which Jesus gathered the tribes of the new Israel and, starting from the triumphant entry into Jerusalem, the Twelve will be the only witnesses of the beginning of the journey of the passion. But they are incapable of bearing the trial: like the crowd, all the disciples, men and women, will abandon him (14:50), and Jesus will go alone toward the cross.

Therefore, from a narrative point of view, the caesura is clear between the first part of the story of the passion, in which, from Gethsemane onward, all the disciples have fled; and the second part, the one with a kerygmatic importance, which goes from the crucifixion to Easter morning, when some of the disciples, that is, the Galilean women, together with all the other women, reappear on the scene. The historical information on those three specific women who "used to follow and provided for him when he was in Galilee" is thus set in a storyline with a strong kerygmatic character: the small group led by Mary Magdalene and the "many others" represent the moment of transition from the story of the Galilean prophet, of which they were eyewitnesses, to the Christian preaching of the death and burial of Jesus of Nazareth.

Mark's passion narrative constitutes the narrative nucleus from which the other two Synoptic evangelists take their cue—not without, however, some significant differences.

Accompanying Jesus: Matthew's Gospel

> Many women were also there, looking on from a distance; they had followed Jesus from Galilee and had provided for him. Among them were Mary Magdalene, and Mary the mother of James and Joseph, and the mother of the sons of Zebedee.
>
> Matt 27:55–56

Like Mark, Matthew also names Mary the Magdalene three times (Μαρία ἡ Μαγδαληνή): at the crucifixion (27:55–56), the burial site (27:61), and the tomb on Easter morning (28:1). He therefore resumes the Marcan tradition of the presence of women at the crucifixion (Mark 15:40–41). As we have already noted, however, the list of the female disciples presents variations not only in names but also in the number of the female disciples.[8] As with Mark, even with Matthew it is not entirely clear whether the women are three or four: it depends on whether Mary (the wife) of James is a different figure from (the) mother of Joseph. Finally, there is the mother of the sons of Zebedee, who takes the place that in Mark was occupied by Salome and who, for Matthew, is an already known character: in 20:20, the evangelist said that it was she who demanded from Jesus a privileged place in the kingdom for her children. Above all, however, Matthew does not follow Mark in the description of the small group of women called by name.

As in Mark, the three nominal references accurately identify three women within a larger group of women who observed ἀπὸ μακρόθεν (from a distance). Matthew, however, attenuates the strength given to their presence by having followed-served Jesus since he was in Galilee, that is, from having taken part from the beginning to his mission. In fact, to say that the three female disciples had followed Jesus from Galilee is quite different from saying that they followed him while he was in Galilee: in Matthew, Mary of Magdala and the other two (or three) seem to have been more companions than disciples in the strict sense. Above all, the combination of the aorist verbal form (ἠκολούθησαν: "followed") and the present participle διακονοῦσαι (serving him) indicate an action that ended in the past and gives an episodic character to the following of the three women. Moreover, unlike Mark, Matthew does not state, as we have already mentioned, that the women followed-served Jesus for the whole time of his Galilean activity, but they followed him from Galilee (ἠκολούθον ἀπὸ τῆς Γαλιλαίας), that is, since Jesus left Galilee. Finally, the links between the description of the role of the Galilean women and the theology of discipleship are much less evident in Matthew than in Mark, since he excludes any reference to the ascent to Jerusalem. This question arises: Could the tradition of Mary of Magdala and the other female Galilean disciples have begun to lose its original significance very early? Did the fact that the community of disciples around Jesus was formed by men *and* women lose value for Matthew and his community? Contrary to appearances, Luke will only strengthen this suspicion.

Freed from Demons: Luke's Gospel

Soon afterwards he went on through cities and villages, proclaiming and bringing the good news of the kingdom of God. The twelve were with him, as well as some women who had been cured of evil spirits and infirmities: Mary, called Magdalene, from whom seven demons had gone out, and Joanna, the wife of Herod's steward Chuza, and Susanna, and many others, who provided for them out of their resources.

Luke 8:1–3

Luke brings some significant variations to the traditions of the female disciples of Jesus at the crucifixion. First, the third evangelist does not name Mary Magdalene and the others at the cross, but only at the burial site and at the empty tomb. It is also true, however, that Luke had previously mentioned a small group of female Galilean disciples in a summary of the mission of Jesus in Galilee (8:1–3). This is only in part two parallel references. But let us proceed in order.

For Mark, as we have seen, the three names of the Galilean women at the crucifixion and burial site are closely linked to an important element of the theology of discipleship in which the themes of following, service, and taking up one's cross are intertwined with each other and are in strict continuity with the words and teachings of Jesus. Concerning this, the three female disciples, who since the beginning had followed and served Jesus, had made the journey with him to Jerusalem, and had witnessed his death until the final word of his burial, are exemplary figures. Above all, they are the undisputed protagonists because they are the only ones on the scene, both of the facts and of their kerygmatic narration.

For Luke, however, the crucifixion is a "spectacle" (θεορία) that is attended even by the crowds (23:48). Beyond its plausibility, this detail is indicative of the orientation that the third evangelist intends to confer on his account of the passion. Through it he claims questions, not only the Christians of the third generation to whom he addresses his Gospel, but, implicitly, even the later ones: to affirm that the confession of faith of the Roman centurion is the background of the penitential journey of the crowd that beats its chest with regret because it grasped the sense of what has happened; and if it returns home in a penitential attitude, it means that the Gospel is for everyone and has a universal reach. According to Luke, a rather indistinct group of "acquaintances" of Jesus and of women—whose names he mentions—are at the crucifixion. It is not easy to understand why. The evangelist prefers to keep this group very fluid, and it is even possible for the Twelve to be part of it, given that he has omitted the episode of their flight. Moreover, the reference to acquaintances clearly evokes the Old Testament, recalling Psalms 37:12 [LXX] and 87:9–10, and favors the theological identification between Jesus's death and that of those just persecuted. Luke, in short, seems less interested in establishing the story of Jesus's death in a historical context, and more in giving it a first symbolic reading.

As for Mary and, more specifically, the other women, the reference to their service completely disappears and the strong reason for the ascent with Jesus to Jerusalem vanishes: more than disciples, the women are just accompanying Jesus. Here, as in the parallel story, unique to Luke, of the women weeping on the way of the cross (23:27), the verb to follow has a generic meaning, since the subject of the action is the crowd. Luke certainly does not intend to superimpose the women who witness the crucifixion over those who lament over him, but for both, the tendency to generalization is clear, and the verb to follow has no other meaning than to accompany. Mary and the others went up to Jerusalem to see what would happen. When it comes exclusively to discipleship of women, then, Luke prefers not to use a pregnant terminology and chooses rather generic and insignificant formulations. Why does he dilute their relevant role in a great mass scene and does not even name them?

According to some scholars, the answer to these questions lies in the fact that the third evangelist, unlike the others, has already spoken of the female disciples during the narration of the mission of Jesus in Galilee, of their travels with Jesus and their diaconate for him (Luke 8:1–3). Indeed, this very text convinced many that Luke had an interest in women. This is far from being the case: although it is true that the third Gospel contains a significantly higher number of texts on women than the others, it is easy to see that this quantitative wealth is paralleled by a clear desire to exclude women from the exercise of the apostolic role. A clear example of this, among others, is provided precisely by the text in question.[9]

In the outline summarizing Jesus's mission in Galilee, Luke inserts a list naming three women who, together with the Twelve, are "with Jesus." Even for Luke, who manifests more than the other Synoptics an interest in the Twelve, the disciples of Jesus are not reducible only to the Twelve, and they are joined by three specific women, named exactly as were the Twelve at the time of the call (6:13–16). They include some women who were cured: "Mary, called Magdalene, from whom seven demons had gone out," as well as "Joanna, the wife of Herod's steward Chuza, and Susanna, and many others, who provided for them out of their resources" (8:2–3). As we can see, the list shows strong differences from those in Mark and Matthew, but partly also with the one that Luke himself inserts at the end of the story of the Easter apparition in which, in addition to Mary Magdalene, there is always Joanna instead of Susanna, and Mary, the mother of James (24:10).

We will return later to the story of the Easter apparition. Mary of Magdala is always in first place, confirming that her name and her role were passed down with veneration. Something unique is said here of her: she was freed from diabolical possession. This news will then echo, as we saw earlier, also in Mark 16:19, and it will have great fortune in patristic and medieval literature: the Western fathers will assimilate the Gospel data by identifying Mary Magdalene with the sinner of Luke 7:36–50 and with Mary of Bethany, sister of Lazarus and Martha, of Luke 10:38–42, John 11:1–45, and John 12:1–8 (see Matt 26:6–13 and Mark 14:3–9). Like Mary, Joanna was a Galilean, the wife of Herod's steward. Luke seems to consider her a prominent figure since, making a clear change to the pre-Marcan tradition, he also adds her name to the list of women at the Easter events. The interest in Herod's household, however, is characteristic of the third Gospel. Of Susanna, there is absolutely nothing said here or elsewhere.

It is therefore assumed that the evangelist has included in the list the names of two women known from his specific environment. Beyond this, what is striking is that Mary and the others no longer exercise, as is the case with Mark, a discipleship and diakonia for Jesus, but, along with many others, they are economic supporters of Jesus's mission and of his disciples. It is very likely that Luke uses here the memory of the Galilean women to make an appeal to the wealthy women of his community, so they would support the ecclesial mission. Indeed, their memory serves to ground and strengthen the exhortation.

Conversely, if it is impossible that some women were part of Jesus's followers, it is unlikely that they were wealthy and had goods available to offer to the itinerant group of disciples of the Galilean. It is a possibility for the Lucan community, which, as we know from repeated exhortations of the evangelist in this regard, also included wealthy women.[10] This is confirmed by the reference to Joanna, wife of Herod's steward. It is difficult to believe that she followed Jesus in his Galilean mission, while it is possible to think that Luke includes her as an example of a convert who made her assets available to the community. To argue, then, based on this information, that Mary Magdalene belonged to a wealthy class and was wealthier than the wife of the king's steward because she is mentioned before her, seems to me to be a fanciful conjecture.

Beyond that, Luke includes in his summary of 8:1–3 a piece of information about the three Galilean women that we find nowhere else: they share the experience of having been liberated from illnesses. It is reasonable to wonder whether the evangelist keeps this information only as a traditional relic or intends to attribute some specific meaning to it. Could it be that, as some think, the experience of healing was the reason for the three Galilean women to follow the Prophet of Nazareth? If so, does the absence of stories of Jesus's direct calling of women find a possible justification in the equivalence between call and healing?

However, for Luke, healing is never a call. On the contrary, the leper (5:14) and the paralytic (5:25) go back to their former life, and Jesus himself explicitly prohibits the Gerasene demoniac, after he healed him, to follow him (8:38–39). The conviction, however widespread, that the reason the Galilean women followed Jesus was their gratitude for the healing is completely groundless. It is not difficult to understand, however, why many insist on the topic of gratitude: when dealing with women, it is always convenient to indulge in sentiment. It is very likely that Luke receives from the tradition the news about Mary "from whom seven demons had gone out," and it is possible that this woman of Magdala had suffered from a serious psychic illness. It is, however, equally possible that, if she followed Jesus from the time of his Galilean ministry up to the moment of the cross, she did it not because she was πάροιστρος (crazy) as suggested by later anti-Christian propaganda,[11] but because she recognized that in the Nazarene's proclamation of the kingdom, her messianic anxiety was finally answered and her eschatological expectation was fulfilled.

Where has this examination of the story of Jesus's death-burial in the three Synoptic Gospels led us? What do they tell us about Mary Magdalene? Some data seem clear to me.

First, as the pre-Marcan passion narrative shows, the memory of the presence of some women at the cross and at the burial site belongs to the most ancient tradition of Jesus. Three (or four) of them were considered disciples of Jesus who had followed him from the beginning of his mission in Galilee until his tragic end in Jerusalem. Mary Magdalene was at the head of the small group of female Galilean disciples.

Second, it is not easy to specify the configuration of the group of disciples who shared Jesus's missionary journeys. However, for centuries an exegesis aimed at establishing the procedures of identification and transmission of authority, with the help of a reductive iconographic tradition, has identified the entire group of disciples following Jesus with the Twelve, thus dramatically altering the reality preserved in the Gospel texts. The symbolic and inclusive value of the number suggests that it refers to all, men and women, who agreed to share with Jesus the cause of the kingdom and thus become part of the new Israel.

In addition, all three evangelists acknowledge the ancient tradition of the female Galilean disciples at Calvary in their accounts of the passion. This means that, even after decades, it was considered important to keep alive the memory of the role played by these women within the group of disciples. Why?

It should also be noted that Matthew and, above all, Luke evaluate the discipleship of Mary differently from Mark. For them, Mary, who was in an important sense more than just a disciple, and, a fortiori, more than the other two women, was, on the path to the passion, accompanying Jesus. Finally, the use made by Luke of the tradition of the women in the summary of the mission of Jesus in Galilee (8:1–3) can help to answer the question why it was important to transmit the memory of these women: the presence of women within the first Christian communities was relevant, and the memory of the female disciples provided an exemplary model of behavior and could thus be used in a parenetic key.

GUARANTOR OF THE CONSTITUTION OF THE COMMUNITY: THE GOSPEL OF JOHN

Meanwhile, standing near the cross of Jesus were his mother, and his mother's sister, Mary the wife of Clopas, and Mary Magdalene.

John 19:25

It is well known that John condenses his narration around individual characters and thus reinforces them, thanks to an accentuated personalization of the situations, narrative intensity, and theological density. He will do the same in the story of the empty tomb and with Mary of Magdala, whom he presents as the recipient of the first apparition of the Risen Lord. We will examine it in detail later. Here we want to pay attention to the use that the Fourth Evangelist makes of the ancient tradition of the presence of the female disciples of Jesus at the crucifixion. What remains is only a reference to Mary Magdalene by name. For John, too, there are three women at the foot of the cross, and he is keen to list them. However, these women are completely different from those in the Synoptics. First, there is "the mother of Jesus," whom John never calls by the name of Mary but always "mother" (see 2:1), and whom Jesus addresses only as γύναι (woman).

There is then Mary, Clopas's wife, the sister of Jesus's mother, and, only at the end, Mary of Magdala. Her tradition is

51

also confirmed, therefore, in the Fourth Gospel. John's interest, however, is no longer in the group of female Galilean disciples. For him, the crucifixion is the place where the new community of disciples is born on the foundation of the exaltation of Jesus on the cross. Along with them there is another figure, "the disciple whom he loved," who plays a particularly important role in John's passion (see 13:23 and 18:15).

If for the Synoptics it was important to guarantee the historicity of the scene of the crucifixion, this was the reason to mention some well-known eyewitnesses. In John, the perspective changes completely, and the main concern is to create the scene of Jesus's death using symbolic elements with a high theological-ecclesial meaning. For him, the cross does not represent a moment of failure in the story of Jesus, but the peak of his glorification. It is a death not only told, but theologically interpreted in close connection with the resurrection. Jesus himself had foretold, "And I, when I am lifted up from the earth, will draw all people to myself" (12:32). Now that he is lifted up, this prophecy is fulfilled, first by constituting the new community of his disciples (19:25–27), the small group of disciples to whom he "gave up" his spirit (19:30).

Nothing is said of Mary of Magdala and, at first sight, it seems that John's interest in her under the cross does not go beyond naming her, in continuity with the primitive tradition. Against this extremely minimalist reading is the opinion of some women exegetes who instead support the identification with Mary Magdalene and "the disciple whom he loved"; the text is not entirely clear in this regard. As commonly believed, the figure of the anonymous "disciple whom he loved" is the one around whose authoritative testimony the tradition of the origin of the Fourth Gospel has developed. Although not part of the group of the Twelve, this disciple had a strictly personal relationship with Jesus and transmitted his memory. Given the role that the Fourth Evangelist will immediately attribute to Mary in the narration of the apparition, the possibility that "the disciple whom Jesus loved" coincides with Mary of Magdala is not entirely far-fetched.

Here, however, I am interested in emphasizing something else. I believe that the mention of those under the cross and the scene of the "entrusting" of the son to the mother and of the mother to the son have strong theological value. The story of the death of Jesus has a strong symbolic character, and each scene has high theological meaning: Why should the evangelist have given to the episode of the mutual delivery of the mother and the beloved disciple a purely sentimental value, as is commonly emphasized? If we exclude the first episode of Jesus's mission, at Cana of Galilee, there is no reference throughout the Fourth Gospel to a relationship between Jesus and his mother, and, even more, to a particularly affective relationship. Why then at the end should he be concerned with entrusting her to a disciple so that, as is maintained, someone can care for her by taking her into their home? Two clues are worth considering. First, the evangelist states that ἀπ'ἐκείνης τῆς ὥρας (from that hour) the disciple took her εἰς τὰ ἴδια (into his own home), using two expressions that, in the rest of the Gospel, have a significant theological weight. The hour of Jesus (ἡ ὥρα) is the moment of his manifestation and of his glorification,[12] and, not surprisingly, the first time that Jesus alludes to its meaning is precisely to correct his mother's expectations (2:4: "Woman, what concern is that to you and to me? My hour has not yet come"). Second, in the Prologue, the lemma εἰς τὰ ἴδια is translated as "what was his own" and even indicates the incarnation of the Word as well as the drama of the rejection of the revelation by the Jewish people (1:11).

Why then, at the solemn moment of the cross, should both these words lose their strong theological sense and express only Jesus's concern that his mother have a place to live, as if he had been living with her or it had been his concern to secure it for her? Once again, it must be noted that, when the Gospel accounts concern women, the history of the interpretation always takes on apologetic qualities or refers to affective or domestic contextualizations.

This remains true even today, even though starting from the fourth century, that is, from the moment of the exaltation of the figure of Mary, another possibility comes to the fore, that of seeing in the mother under the cross the symbol of the Church. The alternative between the domestic hearth and the heavenly throne seems to me completely out of tune within the narrative strategy and the theology of the Fourth Gospel because both possibilities take away from Mary her narrative role: to mark the beginning and fulfillment of the "hour" of the Messiah and represent the continuity between the pre-Easter and post-Easter Israel.

I am convinced that, with the story of the presence of the two disciples at the foot of the cross together with Jesus's mother, the evangelist wants to go much further than Jesus's filial love for his mother. He means to point out the community of those who, coming from Judaism and believing in the resurrection, are in continuity with the historical Jesus, and thus, with Israel of the promise and, at the same time, with the Word Incarnate. John is interested in presenting to his community the moment of its origin. Its foundation is rooted in the cross, that is, when Jesus, with sovereign authority, establishes the reciprocal entrusting of his mother and the "disciple whom he loved," between the mother of the Messiah and the new children "who were born, not of blood or of the will of the flesh or of the will of man, but of God" (John 1:13). Not surprisingly, as we shall see, only from this moment those who believe in him will receive the title of "brothers" (20:17). The claim of the "disciple whom he loved" receives a strong investiture at the foot of the cross: the reciprocal entrusting between the mother and the disciple legitimates the testimony of the "disciple whom Jesus loved." He who, though not part of the group of the Twelve, was nevertheless present at the Last Supper, at the trial and at the cross, has guarded and transmitted an authentic tradition of Jesus. In it the communities to which John addresses his Gospel find their origin and nourishment.

Mary of Magdala, of whom the evangelist has not yet spoken, arrives on the scene under the cross in John as well, as the tradition had handed down. But she witnesses the scene of the "entrusting," from which the life of the community of those who believe in the Risen Lord begins. Shortly thereafter, she will be invested by the Risen Lord himself with the mission to announce the resurrection to the community of disciples and to explain its meaning to them (20:17ff.). Precisely in view of this apostolic investiture, her presence under the cross to assist the foundation of the community of those who believe in the exalted Jesus can only represent a precedent that is in some way necessary. For John, her participation in Jesus's death does not have the value of eyewitness testimony but is rather propaedeutic to the apostolic investiture that she will receive "the first day of the week" in the garden where Joseph of Arimathea and Nicodemus had buried the body of Jesus (19:38ff.). We will examine this in the final part of this study.

In conclusion, therefore, all four Gospels repeat the traditional data: Mary of Magdala, leader of a group of female disciples, is a witness to the death and burial of Jesus.

Each evangelist assumes and modulates this traditional element in his own personal way, starting from its theological-ecclesial perspectives and according to his narrative purpose. Nobody says much about Mary of Magdala, but that also applies to every other character. In no way in fact should the narrative centrality of Jesus be blurred by the characterization of other characters: in the Gospels there is only one protagonist, all the others are functional extras to what the evangelist wants to narrate, declare, assert of him. Mary's evangelical identity is therefore entirely functional: the disciple of Magdala is what she is called to represent, that is, the witness of the death of Jesus and of his burial, in the plurality of meanings that this may entail.

A Historical and Theological Identity

As the trajectory that goes from the Synoptics to John shows, the significance of Mary Magdalene's presence at the foot of the cross of Jesus, rooted in the preservation of a historical fact, changes. For all three Synoptics, Mary is not only present at an event, but she bears witness to the meaning of that event. The kerygmatic character of the stories of the passion is clear evidence of this. The presence of Mary and of the other female disciples at the cross has the strong value of paradigmatic witness to the faith of all those who want to be disciples of the Risen One.

The outline of the historical information on this woman and her discipleship, decidedly pronounced in Mark, however, changes progressively. By involution, as in Matthew, and above all in Luke, Mary is no longer mentioned as a disciple of Jesus in her own right, the leader of the group of female Galilean disciples who had followed and provided for Jesus since the beginning of his mission. By evolution, as in John, Mary is under the cross not only because she was a historical disciple of Jesus, but as a witness of the last will of the crucified Lord, that is, of the constitution of the Easter community. The four passion narratives thus provide us with a clear example of the dual possibility of a strong theological meaning to the discipleship of Mary Magdalene and to her presence at the cross and burial site. One thing, however, is certain: Peter is not under the cross, while Mary is. Neither Peter nor any of the Twelve attend the burial of the Teacher or is at the tomb on Easter morning. Instead, Mary and the other female disciples are there.

Chapter 4

Witness to the Resurrection

AT THE ORIGINS OF THE EASTER FAITH: THE SYNOPTIC GOSPELS

Why should they have been afraid, they who found what
they were looking for?

Pseudo-Jerome (ninth century)

As the events proceed, it becomes increasingly difficult to distinguish between chronology and theological plans in Jesus's resurrection narratives. According to the canonical Gospels, we know that
no one witnessed Jesus's resurrection: it is not narrated as an event
in which we take part, but it is assumed that we experience the consequences, from the discovery of the empty tomb to the individual
and collective experience of the vision of the one who is not to be
sought among the dead because he is alive. The kerygmatic character of the story becomes more and more pronounced. Once again,
and in all four Gospel accounts, Mary Magdalene stands on the
threshold between history and faith. According to the Synoptics,
she stands with the other Galilean female disciples; according to
John, she stands alone.

Between Fear and Memory

The story of the vision of the angel on Easter morning has all
the traits of a divine epiphany. It is a highly structured theological
story. For this reason, in my opinion, the element of the empty
tomb cannot have only apologetic value; that is, it is not told only
to generate amazement and thus prepare for the idea of Jesus's
resurrection. Besides, not even the presence of the women at Jesus's
burial (Mark 15:47ff.) was intended only to substantiate a death

that actually happened. In this regard, the formula of faith of 1 Corinthians 15:3–5 alerts us: the burial has a kerygmatic value. Even in the Gospel accounts, Jesus's burial has a precise relevance, both for Jesus and the disciples. It is the decisive hinge between the before and after of the point of arrival of the earthly parable of the Messiah and the starting point of the parable that leads the Messiah to pass from life to a totally new creation, but also as the point of arrival of the discipleship toward the prophet of Nazareth and the point of departure of the discipleship toward the Risen Christ.

The shattering force of the announcement of the resurrection lies in this passage: that is, that tomb, empty of the body of the Galilean, and visited by the angels of God. The point of intersection between the parable of Jesus of Nazareth and that of the disciples is precisely the female disciples, and particularly Mary of Magdala, who accompany Jesus until the last act of his life and his burial, and are present at the first act of the life of the Risen One, the divine epiphany. For them, the sight of the empty tomb means accepting that Jesus is no longer there (Mark 16:6), but also that no disciple can find him among the dead because he is alive in another way (Luke 25:5).

Specifically, the Marcan story presents the protagonists of Easter morning with a precise and decisive indication for understanding the meaning of the entire situation. In Mark 16:6, the women are described as those who seek Jesus the Nazarene the Crucified One ('Ιησοῦν ζητεῖτε τὸν Ναζαρηνὸν τὸν ἐσταυρωμένον). We will see later that this is also true in John, for whom Mary is the disciple who seeks Jesus (20:15). Unlike John, however, Mark uses the verb ζητέω throughout his Gospel to sanction a negative attitude toward Jesus. The citizens of Capernaum who demand healing (1:38), the family of Jesus who wants to protect him (3:20–21, 31–32), the hostile Pharisees who want a sign from heaven (8:11–13), all those who want him dead (11:18; 12:12; 14:1, 11, 55), and, finally, the female disciples who want to honor his dead body (16:1): they all "seek" him.

Moreover, the tension within the story, which goes from the anxiety of the women seeking those who can help them roll the stone that closes the tomb, to the fright of the vision of the angel, makes clear that the term ζητέω is a prelude to something new that must happen: the Galilean women can no longer search for Jesus, the crucified Nazarene, in the places of his death, for he now precedes his disciples (προάγει ὑμᾶς) in Galilee and there he will be visible as the Risen One. The term προάγω (to precede), which recalls Jesus's prophecy before his passion (14:27: "You will all become deserters; for it is written, / 'I will strike the shepherd, / and the sheep will be scattered'"), opens the story to an ecclesial dimension: Jesus's resurrection marks the refoundation of the community of disciples after the shepherd has been struck and the sheep have been dispersed.

Thus, even if only implicitly, Mark foresees an ecclesiological development of the first Easter epiphany to the women, which is more evident in the other three Gospels.[1] Jesus's resurrection requires to go beyond the scandal of his death that has overwhelmed all the disciples (14:27: πάντες σκανδαλισθήσεσθε) and Peter himself (14:29–30). But it also requires going beyond the desire of the female disciples to do for Jesus what the women of his family should have done, anointing his now lifeless body. For the women, in short, the epiphany determines the beginning of a new type of community of disciples.

In Mark, however, the scene is also dominated by a strong climate of shock and fear: when they enter the tomb, the three female disciples were alarmed at the sight of the angel (ἐξεθαμβήθησαν), the angel encourages them with the invitation to not be alarmed (μὴ ἐκθαμβεῖσθε), but they fled from the tomb because they are full of terror and amazement (εἶχεν γὰρ αὐτὰς τρόμος καὶ ἔκστασις), and the scene ends with a laconic "and they said nothing to anyone, for they were afraid [ἐφοβοῦντο γάρ]" (16:8). In Matthew, however, the tension diminishes and the women leave the tomb "with fear and great joy" (28:8), while in Luke the reference to terror is only a rhetorical device that puts greater emphasis on the words of the angels (24:5).

In Mark, therefore, the terrified silence of the female disciples even seals the Gospel story (16:8).[2] Evidently, no one believes that the silence of Mary Magdalene and the other women can be taken literally: if the women kept silent, where would the same Gospel of Mark come from? The evangelist certainly cannot think that his readers are so radically lacking in common sense that they are unable to grasp the need to use literary stratagems to give theological strength to the story.

However, their silence remains ambiguous. Especially in cultures where women were restricted if not banned from speaking in public, antithetical meanings could be given to silence. On the one hand, the evangelist might want to defend the story from the suspicion of unreliability, given that women are the ones who talk. In Luke, this becomes clear: the apostles consider the account of the women an "idle tale" (24:11), and the two disciples of Emmaus confirm the scarce credibility the community of disciples gives to the women's account (24:22–23).

Mark, on the other hand, may have used their silence not only because it is literally very effective but, above all, because theologically it is very pregnant: the passion story begins at Bethany with the silence of the woman who prophetically anoints the body of Jesus (14:3–9), and it now ends with a silence that prepares, equally prophetically, for the gospel of the resurrection. Of the former it is said that "wherever the good news is proclaimed in the whole world, what she has done will be told in remembrance of her" (Mark 14:9); the paschal vision of an angel to Mary the Magdalene and to the other women represents the indispensable condition for the proclamation of the Gospel to begin: "go, tell his disciples and Peter that he is going ahead of you to Galilee; there you will see him, just as he told you" (16:7). From Galilee to Galilee: it is the messianic trajectory and the trajectory of discipleship. The Galilean female disciples are those who, together with Jesus, first, and, on the mandate of the Risen Lord, afterward, guarantee its realization.

To decide on a meaning to attribute to the Marcan motif of the women's silence remains, however, difficult. In any case, it is a fact that the testimony of Mary and of the other female disciples has guaranteed the elaboration of the Easter faith and of the first kerygma of the resurrection. From this point of view, Luke is even more explicit because he explains the theological contribution of the Galilean female disciples. For the evangelist, to seek for the Living One means first to remember what he said and did when he was alive: "Remember how he told you, while he was still in Galilee" (24:6). Although, for the third evangelist, the preaching of the Gospel does not actually start from Galilee but Jerusalem, the announcement of the resurrection entails the memory of the history of the Nazarene.

The female disciples are therefore the receivers of memory. For Mary and for the other women, as we have said, the tomb represents the place where the search of the disciples radically changes in perspective because it is the place of the divine epiphany, and the absence becomes prophecy: there, where Jesus the Nazarene, the Crucified One, passes from death to life, Mary and the other Galilean women pass from the historical discipleship of the prophet of Nazareth to being disciples of the Risen One. From the historical-theological point of view, this is a decisive but extremely delicate passage: faith in the resurrection can in fact result in a dangerous mythological shift. The genesis of the Easter faith, but also the guarantee that it does not become a myth among others, is therefore in the memory of what Jesus said and did. Of this, Mary and the other female disciples, who already "used to follow him and provided for him when he was in Galilee" (Mark 15:41; see also Luke 8:1–2), have been the guarantors.

This last point calls for further scrutiny. In the early Christian centuries, the fathers were, indeed, the great theorists of the incarnation, but well before them, what allowed the Christian announcement to not fade into the myth of a Christ without Jesus was the memory of the Galilean female disciples: "'Remember how he told you, while he was still in Galilee'....Then they remembered his words." (Luke 24:6–8). Within the process of elaboration of the Easter faith, of the missionary proclamation, and of the ecclesial parenesis, the recovery of the traditional material on Jesus and the composition of the four Gospel narratives represent a decisive inversion, of course. Not only the death and resurrection, but also the figure and the work of Jesus of Nazareth, is vigorously placed at the center of the kerygmatic announcement. The Pauline "even though we once knew Christ from a human point of view, we know him no longer in that way" (2 Cor 5:16) had guaranteed access to the Easter faith even to all those who, albeit coming after the historical events of Jesus and of his first disciples, had believed in him. Now, however, affirming the close continuity between the kerygma of the resurrection and the person of Jesus guarantees that the Christian proclamation does not become the mythological foundation of a new ideology of salvation. Can it be then that the Gospel accounts of the apparition to the women on the morning of Easter tell us that it is precisely to the women—to the Galilean female disciples first, and to the female believers of the second generation—that we owe the preservation of the historical memory of Jesus and its recovery within the Gospel redactions? "'Remember how he told you, while he was still in Galilee'....Then they remembered his words" (Luke 24:6–8).

Women and Faith in the Resurrection

At this point it is legitimate to ask why Mary of Magdala and the other Galilean female disciples were able to perceive the experience of Easter morning as an announcement of the resurrection. This is tantamount to wondering about the conception of death and life after death that was part of their experience as Jewish women because it was related to their beliefs and their religious customs. Is it enough to affirm that the presence of the female disciples at the tomb on Easter morning was due to their affection for their Teacher, or dictated by their social duties toward the dead?

Personally, I believe that precisely those tasks, together with all the others associated with their social roles, have prompted a reflection on death on their part and an openness to waiting for the resurrection of the dead. This is exactly what made them able to formulate and express, before others, the announcement of the resurrection: their "caring for the dead" made the women who had followed Jesus able to understand the death of their Teacher as an event from which his resurrection begins. However, in the biblical tradition, it is possible to recognize a very particular connection between the faith of women and the question of death and resurrection.

We know that the idea of immortality does not belong to the Israelite faith from the beginning: "we are like water spilled on the ground, which cannot be gathered up" (2 Sam 14:14).[3] Death has a definitive value, it is a situation in front of which even hope does not make any sense. Regarding this, however, the time of exile marks a decisive passage that involves the individualization of relations with God[4] and the expectation of the fulfillment of God's judgment. In the latter days before Christ, death then acquires moral qualities as the fruit of sin,[5] the idea of death acquires depth and theological relevance, and the hypothesis of the resurrection of the dead begins to emerge. Never has it been conceived as a simple return to life of a corpse, nor, even less, has it been assimilated to the concept of immortality. In the future kingdom of God, there will not be death and even past generations will enjoy a new creation: in the end, the hope of the resurrection thus comes to coincide with the ultimate fulfillment of what God has promised to accomplish for those whom were chosen.

The idea of the resurrection of the dead, however, does not entirely impose itself. From the Gospels it is clear, for example, the opposition to it by the Sadducees as shown by the controversy, pushed to paradox, that they undertake with Jesus around the institute of the levirate, widely practiced in the Middle Eastern world and, though not without problems,[6] even in Israel (see Mark 12:18–27; Matt 22:23–33; Luke 20:27–39). Moreover, the Christian preaching on Jesus's resurrection has always had to face, both in the Jewish and in the pagan world, the existence or not of the necessary yet insufficient premise of faith in the resurrection of the dead. Regarding this, the apostolic preaching of Peter and John (Acts 4:2) and of Paul (Acts 23:6, 8) clashed with rejection.[7]

The biblical tradition thus reveals that the assumption of awareness of the possibility of the resurrection after death has led to a slow and uneven process. But what interests us here is that only female figures are the expression of this awareness, and therefore they acquire an emblematic character: Rachel and the mother of the seven Maccabees, in the Old Testament, and in the New Testament, Martha.

The matriarch Rachel represents for Israel the icon of hope in the resurrection, understood as a metaphor for the reconstitution of Israel. Her role as a matriarch of Israel immediately appears to be more closely related to death than to life, since she dies by giving birth to Jacob's last sons, and her figure helps to understand why she only, and not the other matriarchs, has received from tradition such a strong symbolic character.[8] Jacob will bury her not at Machpelah, along with the other patriarchs and matriarchs, but alone, along the road that, after the painful years of exile, leads

Israel finally back to Canaan.[9] Even today, Rachel's tomb attracts, among the various pilgrims, especially infertile women who wish to overcome sterility. Traditionally, this tomb becomes the sign of the end of times of tribulation and anguish and must remain so until the end of the exile, even until the resurrection of the dead. Considered by now the mother of all the sons of Jacob, even of those conceived by her sister Leah, Rachel would have comforted them when, returning from exile, they would have passed before her tomb, and, crying for them, she would bear their afflictions and would have secured her help. Inconsolable in the face of the pain of her children, she is the only one who can endure the infinite duty of consolation. And she, who can only accept the consolation of the Messiah, makes the waiting for the messianic era heart-wrenching with her weeping.

There is something extraordinarily powerful in this image that, for this very reason, cannot be separated from the religious-historical experience and end into a pure abstraction or a rhetorical figure, nor can it be forced into the confines of an individual identity. Rachel-Israel in fact gives substance to the relationship with death by the people of the covenant. And the rereading made by Jeremiah 31:15ff. establishes the importance of the intersection between the understanding of death and the experience of Jewish women. Assimilated to exile, death foresees a return and Rachel's cry finds consolation:

> Keep your voice from weeping,
>   and your eyes from tears;
> for there is a reward for your work,
>   says the LORD:
> they shall come back from the land of the enemy.
>   (Jer 31:16)

That is why for Matthew, on the threshold of the messianic era, it will once again be the memory of Rachel who mourns her children that acts as a watershed moment between the old and the new era. Nor is it a case that the rabbis assimilate Rachel's womb to the tombs from which the resurrection will begin. The Targum states that God holds four keys in his hand: the key to the rain with which he opens the sky, the key to nourishment because he opens his hand and feeds every living thing, the key to life with which he opens Rachel's womb, and the key to the tombs that he promised to open.[10]

The words of the mother of the Maccabees are, however, clear signs that the idea of resurrection matures thanks to the experience of persecution and martyrdom, and the hope in the individual resurrection after death appears to be the natural outlet of the primitive theology of retribution: How is it possible that God does not reward those who gave their lives to remain faithful to the law? The one who translates into daily experience the prophetic word that opens to the hope of the resurrection of the dead is once again a woman and, once again, a mother of Israel: Daniel's oracle promised that "many of those who sleep in the dust of the earth shall awake" (12:2), and the mother of the seven Maccabees encourages her children in the extreme trial of martyrdom by appealing to faith in the resurrection. In this text, the eschatological reference is missing, although it is present in Daniel 12, but the resurrection, described as the destiny of the seven brothers, is realized immediately after death, in the heavenly world. De-eschatologized, the idea of resurrection is, however, connected with the themes of the *passio iusti* and martyrdom, themes that have influenced the circles of the first Judaism and therefore also the disciples of Jesus to the point of explicitly inspiring the Christian narration of Jesus's passion. The matriarch Rachel and the mother of the Maccabean martyrs are then two keystones in the process of developing of faith in the resurrection of the dead and establish the conditions for faith in the resurrection of Jesus of Nazareth. They are two mothers and necessarily so. Life originates from mothers, and the experience of motherhood, as a theological place for the elaboration of faith in the God of election and creation, represents a substantial premise for postulating faith, not in immortality, but in the resurrection.

Beyond their actual historical role, these two women figures are both mothers of Israel because they have a decisive influence on the faith of the fathers, prompting it to go beyond the theology of Israel's historical election up to the belief in the resurrection of the dead as intrinsic consequence of both the covenant (Rachel) and creation (the mother of the Maccabees).

Even Martha, the one whom "Jesus loved" together with her sister and brother Lazarus (John 11:5), is the only one among all the disciples of Jesus who has come to know how to receive the revelation of the resurrection of the Messiah from Jesus. She also confirms the very special bond that binds, in the Scriptures, the faith of women to the great question of death and resurrection. The significant parallel with the confession of Peter on the Lake Tiberias is, from this point of view, very eloquent. The dialogue between Martha and Jesus, which prepares for the final christological confession, has as its object the resurrection. Indeed, to be more precise, it has to do with the belief in the resurrection of the dead as a necessary, though not sufficient, preamble to accept the revelation of Jesus and to translate it into an affirmation of christological faith. To Jesus's assurance that the future of resurrection awaits his dead brother, Martha responds, "I know that he will rise again in the resurrection on the last day" (John 11:24). Martha's affirmation represents the precondition for the revelation of the coincidence between Jesus and eternal life (11:25–26: "I am the resurrection and the life. Those who believe in me, even though they die, will live, and everyone who lives and believes in me will never die. Do you believe this?") and for the solemn confession of faith: "Yes, Lord, I believe that you are the Messiah, the Son of God, the one coming into the world" (11:27).

We may perhaps come to say something even more precise if we ask what was to be the content of the messianic expectations of the Jewish women who were part of the following of Jesus. I draw here on an interesting study by Luca Arcari, who also considers Judaism of the first century from a gender perspective.[11] Starting from the specificity of Luke's presentation of the angels' announcement to the women, Arcari examines the Jewish presuppositions of a proto-Christian Christology centered on the "Son of Man." In fact, the angels say to the female disciples, "Why do you look for the living among the dead? He is not here, but has risen. Remember how he told you, while he was still in Galilee, that the Son of Man must be handed over to sinners, and be crucified, and on the third day rise again" (Luke 24:5–7).

Based on the belief that each symbol must be taken into consideration as an instrument of self-definition and thus reveals the worldview expressed by the communities that employ it, Arcari examines the self-definition process put in place by some Jewish groups and proto-Christians using the so-called feminine symbolism. It may not be surprising, in his view, that the Jewish aesthetic-visionary vein has favored the development of that particular kerygmatic announcement of which women become spokespersons in many of the proto-Christian traditions, relying also on that universalistic tendency that seems to be the fundamental presupposition of authority related to the ecstatic experience. The experience of the resurrection narrated by Luke is nothing more than the account of a true vision on the part of women,[12] an account that leads to a "real" understanding of what Jesus had previously said. Nor can it be held that, later, in the Christian communities that will have a liminal location, the ecstatic or apocalyptic vision will often be linked to groups in which women play a role that is anything but marginal. Perhaps, much more will have to be investigated on the relationship between women, their beliefs and their expectations, and the proto-Christian "apocalyptic" kerygma.

It seems to me, however, that, based on what has been said so far, it is entirely possible to suppose that the female disciples of Jesus, if they had followed him during his Galilean activity, were awaiting the kingdom of God and were therefore more prepared and willing to make their own the faith in the resurrection of their Teacher. Their familiarity of Jewish women with death and their faith in the resurrection of the dead meant that, first, for them the resurrection was a plausible event and, consequently, a possible experience. They knew very well, like the mothers of Israel, that at the coming of the Messiah, Rachel's weeping would be consoled and the expectation of the mother who trusted in the Lord even at the time of the hardest trial would be fulfilled with the immediate resurrection of her children.

True, it does not appear in any way that Mary of Magdala was a mother, nor does it appear likely that Martha had children. The shift of the relations from biological to symbolic level, however, has been one of the cornerstones of Jesus's preaching from the beginning. His statement is emblematic: "Whoever does the will of God is my brother and sister and mother" (Mark 3:35), but also the blessedness that contrasts with the exclamation of the woman in the crowd (Luke 11:27–28: "'Blessed is the womb that bore you and the breasts that nursed you!' But he said, 'Blessed rather are those who hear the word of God and obey it!'").

For the Galilean female disciples, the angelic vision on Easter morning meant passing, as for Martha, from the expectation of the resurrection of the Teacher on the last day to the experience of the first day after the Sabbath from which the new creation began. And these were the "mothers" of the faith in the resurrection: if, on a symbolic level, the Twelve represent the reconstitution of the people around the eschatological patriarchs, what prevents us from supposing that the Galilean female disciples understood their discipleship in line with the matriarchs of Israel? Of course, we must limit ourselves to supposing it because, as always, what has been told has helped to legitimize a practice of consolidation and institutionalization for the role of male disciples, but of exclusion for women disciples.

An Unresolved Question

To fully appreciate the extent of the fact that, for the Synoptic narratives, faith in the resurrection begins with the Easter epiphany to the female disciples, it is necessary once again to establish an oppositional comparison with the formula of faith of 1 Corinthians 15:3–8. First, we must make a preliminary observation. True, in the formula there is no mention of women. However, we can legitimately ask whether, as we have already observed, the reference to the Twelve has no numerical value, but a symbolic one, and therefore whether it has an inclusive, and nondiscriminatory meaning.[13] Paul himself, on the other hand, shows that he does not consider the Twelve as an exclusive "apostolic college" since he immediately after mentions an apparition τοῖς ἀποστόλοις πᾶσιν (to all apostles), thus wanting, on the one hand, to establish a precise connection between the experience of the vision and apostolic service and, on the other hand, to legitimize, precisely on the basis of his experience of a vision, his own status as an apostle.[14] Second, it would be quite ridiculous to think that an apparition πεντακοσίοις ἀδελφοῖς ἐφάπαξ (to more than five hundred brothers) of which, moreover, οἱ πλείονες μένουσιν ἕως ἄρτι (most of whom are still alive) should be understood in a strictly masculine sense: Jesus's tomb was not on Mount Athos! Neither the most archaic testimony (v. 5) nor the list that follows it allow us to exclude altogether that it was known that in the early days after Jesus's death even some women had also participated in the enthusiastic phenomena of "visions" of the Risen One.

Explicitly, however, no mention of a woman or a group of women is present in the list of apparitions of the Risen One that accompany the kerygmatic formula resumed by Paul in 1 Corinthians 15. Whether the whole list is traditional or some additions are due to Paul himself, as many believe, does not matter; the fact, however, that no mention is given to the female disciple is a significant indicator. The first transmission of the Easter kerygma would have taken place through a chain of exclusively male testimonies ranging from Peter to five hundred "brothers." Is it possible that neither Paul nor the Judeo-Christian community from which he receives this formula were aware of the ancient traditions of the presence of the women on Calvary and of their first testimony of the resurrection?

Yet, Paul himself proves to have known apostles who preceded him in the mission, including a woman, Junia (Rom 16:7), or to know that a great apostolic service to the community of Rome was carried out by some women like Mary, Tryphaena, Tryphosa, and Persis (Rom 16:6–12).[15] And it is always Paul who believes that apostolic mandate and missionary effort are founded and receive their legitimacy from the personal encounter with the Risen One.

It is possible, therefore, that it was not Paul himself who censured the list of the apparitions of 1 Corinthians 15, and wholly plausible instead to believe that he had already received it as an element of tradition. But then we must conclude that the censorship of the traditions on the women had already occurred, and very soon, in the Judeo-Christian community to which it is possible to trace the formula in question. Is this also a symptom of the gap between "real" history and "official" history that, until recent historiography, has always penalized women?

To proceed, we must do so in small steps. First of all, in all three Synoptic redactions and, in a different way, also in John, the apparitions of the morning of Easter, be they of a "young man, dressed in a white robe" (Mark 16:5), or "an angel" (Matt 28:2), or "two men in dazzling clothes" (Luke 24:4), or even of Jesus himself (John 20:14), are described as women's experiences. Second, it should be noted that they are, however, always functional to others: to "his disciples and Peter," for Mark (16:7); for Matthew, "his disciples" (28:7) or "my brothers" (28:10); "to the eleven and to all the rest," for Luke (24:9). Thus, even the account of the empty tomb, such as those of Paul's vocation (Gal 1:15ff.) or of the choice of Matthias (Acts 1:21ff.), follows the paradigm of the apostolic call: faith in the resurrection is always in view of an announcement and a mission. In John this will be made evident with the explicit sending of Mary to the disciples. In the Gospel accounts, then, the focus of apostolic investiture is not placed on the prerogatives or qualities of those who receive it, but on the recipients of the mission, which are both men and women. One cannot doubt that terms like *disciples* or *brothers* should be understood in an inclusive sense.[16]

Here is the first big difference between the Gospel accounts and the formula of 1 Corinthians 15: instead of being focused on the recipients of the Easter proclamation, the formula insists on the recipients of the apparitions of the Risen Christ who, thanks to an operation put in place for the reconstitution of the group of the Twelve (see Acts 1:12–13), all have become, strictly, men. In short, the formula seems to respond to the need to legitimize the tradition rather than to present its genesis. Above all, it is totally lacking in a missionary perspective.

It should be also recognized that for all three Synoptics the angelic manifestation to the women is a moment of crisis because, as it is said in various ways, it creates uncertainty. Is it just a literary device that allows the final storylines to follow one another in a dramatic crescendo? It is possible. However, especially for Luke, it seems that the credibility of the Easter experiences and their ecclesial legitimacy are delicate issues. Even the experience of the two of Emmaus, after all, seems to find its legitimacy only from the apparition to Peter (24:34).

In this regard, it is likely that two criteria have gradually been imposed. First of all, the passage from a vision of an angel, centered on the proclamation of the resurrection, at the apparition of the Risen Christ himself, and second, the passage from individual experiences, such as that to Simon, mentioned only in Luke 24:34 or the one narrated, again by Luke, to the two disciples on their way to Emmaus (24:13–35), to the solemn apparitions to the entire community gathered around the Eleven, who, more often than not, have a precise liturgical character. As we have already observed, it should also be recalled that the different cultures of the time recognized the testimony of women as almost worthless, and it cannot be surprising that it created, therefore, suspicion and disbelief. Above all, however, the theme of unbelief triggers a strong narrative tension that results in and resolves itself in the solemn final apparitions to the liturgically reunited church.

Even from the historical point of view, however, the motive for the doubt has its own reason. Except for the original ending of Mark, that is to say for the oldest of the Easter stories, doubt occupies the space between the experience of the women—finding the empty tomb, epiphany, and proclamation of the resurrection—and the subsequent apparitions of Jesus: as if the immediacy of the visionary claim of the women had to be followed by the time of a pondered search. The second ending of Mark (16:9–13), in which the memory of the protophany to Mary of Magdala is recovered, reiterates that when she "went out and told those who had been with him, while they were mourning and weeping...when they heard that he was alive and had been seen by her, they would not believe it."

Luke, then, increases the dose given that the words of women "seemed to them as an idle tale, and they did not believe them" (24:11). In Matthew, however, the reason for doubt accompanies the reaction of the "eleven disciples" (28:11). In different terms, John lastly confirms the need for an intermediate time between the experience of the empty tomb and the birth of faith in the resurrection: it takes the necessary time to understand "the scripture, that he must rise from the dead" (20:9). It should not be forgotten that Luke develops all this within the time of the forty days between the resurrection and the ascension, when the Risen Lord himself instructs the disciples: it is the intermediate time of the "disciple pedagogy" and of the elaboration of the doctrine of the Spirit and of eschatology achieved.

This is, in my opinion, a substantial fact that is usually not given much relevance: initially, the announcement of the resurrection is expressed in prophetic-visionary tones and only after a certain time acquires the character of testimony of an experience of apparition. According to the Synoptics, the women are the recipients of an announcement and a promise: Jesus no longer belongs to the sphere of death, but his relationship with the disciples continues because he will be seen alive by them in Galilee (Mark 16:6; Matt 28:7). The experience of the female disciples is thus visionary and charismatic, and starting from it the transmission of a new perspective of hope begins.

It takes a certain amount of time, however, for the announcement of the resurrection to take the form of the objective testimony of an event and be configured as a true apparition of the Risen One. Above all, it is worth repeating, it is important that it takes place during the communal liturgical meeting (Luke 24:33–49 and John 20:19–23, 24–28), and thus acquires symbolic character. Within this process, of which we know neither the times nor the ways because in each of the four Gospels it takes place in different ways and assumes specific theological qualities, the awareness that resurrection and apparitions coincide emerges: Jesus is risen because he has appeared, and he appeared because he is risen.

Is it therefore possible to suppose that the women disappear from the tradition when the story becomes "official," as in the case of the formula resumed by Paul in 1 Corinthians 15? The explicit gender restriction enunciated in Acts 1:21 certainly makes us think so. On the other hand, John's account of the protophany of the Risen One to Mary of Magdala, not only declared as that of Peter in Luke 24:34, nor just formalized in a list, like those of 1 Corinthians 15, but narrated and strongly elaborated theologically can be a clear confirmation in this sense. We will explore this point more in depth later. There, where the women count within the community, the tradition of the apparition of the Risen Lord in person to one who was considered the leader of the group of female disciples is preserved and handed down, while 1 Corinthians 15 can be considered a text that signals a process that will decisively determine the history of the Christian churches: the downplaying of the original form of the testimony of the resurrection, rendered in ecstatic and apocalyptic terms and, with it, the progressive marginalization of women from the organization of the churches, already begun in the early Judeo-Christian communities.

1 Corinthians 15 attests, therefore, that men soon become the stronghold of a faith now well defined, while the female disciples are remembered as the protagonists of the initial moment of a process that gives rise to the Easter faith. A confused, enthusiastic, uncertain, and questionable moment, likely. Decisive, however, because it establishes that no kerygma is possible, no preaching is genuinely Christian if we forget the memory of what Jesus of Nazareth said and did "when he was in Galilee." And the continuity of the memory is guaranteed by the female disciples.

After all, this is what was announced by Jesus himself at the inaugural moment of his Easter itinerary, that is, during the supper in Bethany, when he establishes a precise connection between the prophetic intelligence of a female disciple and evangelization: "Truly I tell you, wherever the good news is proclaimed in the whole world, what she has done will be told in remembrance of her" (Mark 14:9). Anonymous as she is, does not the woman of the anointing at Bethany attest that Jesus's female disciples played an irreplaceable role of connection between the Jewish expectations, the preaching of Jesus, his Easter, and the proclamation of the Gospel throughout the world?

Paul, perhaps, does not know the narrative traditions of Jesus's death and resurrection and, as we know, he is increasingly more interested in the event than in the meanings that it receives from the narrative of its development. Certainly, concerned about legitimizing his experience of the Risen Lord and his apostolic mandate, he prefers to add his own version to a chain of apparently strictly formulated apparitions, only to men. And, in this way, he relaunches, attributing to it the character of *paradosis*, that is, of an established tradition, and that, as such, must be transmitted, a formula that would otherwise have remained the heritage of Judeo-Christian believers of some Palestinian communities who have expressed from the outset the content of their own Easter faith in a form that was soon recognized as a norm for the presentation of the Christian proclamation.[17] Paul, however, certainly could not have imagined that by using his apostolic authority, the theology of the great

Church would have then rooted its own vision of the ecclesiastical order on the conviction that apparitions of the Risen Lord and apostolic mandate had to be considered exclusive prerogative of men, thus completely eclipsing the testimony of the Synoptic evangelists. And even more, as we shall see, that of the Gospel of John.

APOSTLE OF CHRIST: THE GOSPEL OF JOHN

Just as before he [Jesus] had made her the evangelist of his resurrection, so now he made her the apostle of his ascension to the apostles—a worthy recompense of grace and glory, the first and greatest honor, and a reward commensurate with all her services.

Rabanus Maurus, *The Life of Saint Mary Magdalene*, chap. 27

We have already said this at the beginning: if the formula of traditional faith that Paul resumed in 1 Corinthians 15:3ff. originated in the community of John, it probably would have sounded like this: "In fact, I have transmitted to you, first of all, what I have also received, that is, that Christ died for our sins according to the Scriptures, and that he was buried, and that he rose again on the third day according to the Scriptures, and that he appeared to Mary of Magdala, and then to the Twelve." But history, as we know, is not based on speculations. However, insofar as it is inevitable that every historical reconstruction is ideologically oriented, today it is no longer possible to carry out historical research that deals only with the winners and the majorities and then eliminates the defeated and the minorities from official history.[18] This is a criterion that is absolutely fundamental for the whole history of women and very valid for the birth of faith in Jesus's resurrection.

In an essay that appeared when the question of the women in the Gospel texts and, especially, in the Easter stories, began to capture the interest of the great exegetes, François Bovon[19] recalls that critical research on the resurrection distinguishes two types of narration, the "empty tomb" type, in which women are present, and the "apparition" type, of which only the male disciples are the beneficiaries. He also polemically notes that, since the apparition of the Risen One to a woman does not fit into either of these two categories, many exegetes conclude that the three evangelical testimonies (Matt 28:8–11; Mark 16:9; John 20:16) regarding the apparition to Mary Magdalene are late and imaginary. Even science is not without prejudices!

Harshly contesting that this story manifests a popular and legendary character, Bovon believes that, even if it is not easy to re-create it, behind John 20:1–18 and Matthew 28:9–10 lies a tradition, perhaps late, but that manifests a clear necessity, if not really canonical, at least ecclesial. Like all other stories of apparitions, it reflects a precise ecclesial claim. Every early Christian group found in fact its raison d'être and its dignity as a people of God in an apparition of the Risen Lord to its first leader. John 20:1–18 clearly shows the communitarian importance of the discipleship of a woman, better yet, her apostolic investiture. The first task that the exegetical community had to deal with was therefore that of restoring the presence of the women in the Gospel texts to history, at least as much as that of other characters. Of course, we have already noted that those on the empty tomb are stories of proclamation, not of apparition. The Easter angelophanies to the women on Easter morning and the stories of apparition of the Risen Christ to the assembled community are different in character. Between one and the other, we find, with all its uniqueness, the story of the apparition of the Risen One to Mary of Magdala on the very morning of Easter.

If we exclude in fact the apparition to the two of Emmaus and those to the assembled community, in none of the New Testament texts is described an apparition of the Risen One to one of his disciples, either male or female, not even to Peter. Apparitions are mentioned in declarative formulas; they are attested and asserted, not narrated, except for the case of John's account of the apparition to Mary of Magdala (20:1, 11–18). Traces of it remain also in the ending of Matthew (28:8–11) and is resumed in the second ending of Mark, a later one (16:9), as evidence of some difficulty in ignoring it altogether.

Is it possible to believe, as Elisabeth Schüssler Fiorenza[20] did, that the early Christian churches lived the legitimacy of apostolicity in a conflictual way? In which case, if it has survived in both the Mattean and Marcan tradition, as well as the Johannine one, the tradition of Mary Magdalene's primacy must have had considerable force, even if it entered competition with that of Peter. It is difficult to go beyond the hypothesis, obviously, even if, given the weight that prejudices have had on ancient and modern exegetes, we can legitimately conclude that in the early Christian centuries it was not entirely easy to be able to accredit the testimonies of women and on women.

But then, this should make us reflect on the strength some narrative traditions should have if, despite the prejudices, they have been preserved and, at least in part, also transmitted. No one, however, witnessed the apparition of the Risen Lord to Mary of Magdala as no one witnessed that to Paul on the road to Damascus; yet, no one has ever dismissed the latter as imaginary. This does not mean, of course, to historicize the narrative elements of the apparition stories that, especially when it comes to communicating extraordinary experiences, verge on the legendary. But, at the basis of a story with mythical overtones, there can well be a historical experience that motivates, above all, its preservation and transmission.

It is a fact, however, that later, the apparition to Mary of Magdala does not find room into the "master story," even if it is not completely relegated to the legendary. It remains alive for what it is, in a sort of marginal history, which runs parallel to the one officially told. Reading, for example, the *Life of Saint Mary Magdalene* by Rabanus Maurus, a Benedictine monk who lived in the eighth and ninth centuries, it can be inferred that, even centuries after the time of composition of the Gospel of John, the awareness of the significance and value of John's account of the protophany to Mary had not been completely lost. Rabanus Maurus's text deserves to be cited at least in part for the lucid clarity with which he describes the figure of Mary of Magdala and her ecclesial role:

> She knew the friendly voice, she sensed the accustomed gentleness when he called her "Mary" in his usual manner....Hearing this, Mary doubted no longer, but believed in Christ. From hearing the dear voice of the Lord and from seeing his beloved face, she drew faith...and she believed without doubt that she saw Christ, the Son of God, who was truly God, and whom she had loved while

he lived. She believed that the one she had seen die had truly risen from the dead, and that he whom she had placed in the sepulcher was truly equal to God the Father. At last the Saviour was convinced that the love he had before taken such pleasure in had never ceased to burn in the breast of his first servant and special friend, and he knew (he from whom no secret is hidden) that he had ascended to the Father in the heart of his perfume-maker. Just as before he had made her the evangelist of his resurrection, so now he made her the apostle of his ascension to the apostles—a worthy recompense of grace and glory, the first and greatest honor, and a reward commensurate with all her services....Mary, seeing herself elevated by the Son of God, her Lord and Saviour, to such a high position of honor and grace; seeing herself favored with the first and the most privileged of his appearances...could not do otherwise than exercise the apostolate with which she had been honored....Mary announced to her fellow apostles the good news of the Messiah: "I have seen the Lord," and prophesied of the ascension: "And he said these words to me: 'I ascend to my Father and to your Father.'"[21]

In fact, Rabanus Maurus only comments *ad litteram* on John's account of the first apparition of the Risen One on Easter morning. So, let us now look at some of its significant features.

From Before to After

As for the Synoptic narratives, even for John, the tomb is not an element without theological significance and should not be considered solely as a literary device with apologetic purposes, useful to underline that death is without return. In fact, something takes place in the tomb, something theologically relevant both for Jesus and for the disciples.

For the Nazarene, the Crucified One, the tomb is the place of the new creation, that is, the passage from death to life. Even for the disciples—or, better, for the female disciples—the tomb is a place with strong theological symbolism because there, for them, is the passage from the historical discipleship toward the Galilean prophet to the discipleship toward the Risen Christ who ascended to the Father.

The tomb is the place where the status of disciples of the Galilean women, as we have seen, radically changes in perspective and opens the past to the future and the future to the past. This happens thanks to the divine epiphany, which is the prelude to the encounter with the Risen One of the community, in the Synoptics, and thanks, in John, to the apparition of the Risen Lord to Mary of Magdala.

Suffice it to say here that, in the story of the episode (John 20:1, 11–18), two different ways of relating to the tomb are interwoven, which implies the passage between the "before" and the "after" for the Messiah, yes, but also for the female disciple. For this reason, in the first instance, the story must be examined in its original narrative unity, excluding verses 2–12, which interrupt its continuity.[22] We will examine them later because even if they create a clear narrative break, nonetheless, they bring some interesting elements of clarification.

Let us therefore consider, first, the part of the story that sees Mary as the sole protagonist (vv. 1, 11–18). Although John, unlike the Synoptics, did not mention earlier the presence of the female disciples at the burial site, Mary knows that Jesus's body was laid down there. She wants to see it because it is the only way to continue to be a disciple. She does not have to perform any other task because, according to John, the preparation of the body for the burial with scented aromas had already been done by Joseph of Arimathea and Nicodemus (19:39). All that is left for her is grief and crying.

It is not difficult to believe that, at first, that could have been the reaction of the female disciples to the death of Jesus and that John considers precisely that context of mourning as the intimate place of the divine epiphany: two angels in white, sitting one at the head and the other at the feet, where the body of Jesus had been lying, signal the passage now completed (20:12). This is without a word, because the evangelist continues to pursue the logic of signs, so important in the theology of the Fourth Gospel: even the resurrection, the sign par excellence, remains mute, ambiguous, until it is illuminated by a direct revelation by the Christ of God and until there is the recognition of his messianic condition.

A Disciple Who Seeks

That the main theme of the story is the question of the post-Easter discipleship is evident from two elements. From the very beginning, Mary is exemplarily presented as the disciple who "seeks" Jesus. To the verb ζητέω (to seek) is given here a precise christological emphasis, as in Jesus's polemical reactions toward the chief priests and the Pharisees (7:34, 36; 8:21) or in the farewell speech of the Master from his disciples (13:33). But here it also refers openly, above all for the interrogative form of the verb, to the first word addressed by Jesus to his first two disciples (1:38), or to the question that Jesus three times provocatively addresses to the guards who came to the Garden of Gethsemane to arrest him, and which is a prelude to an explicit christological revelation (18:4, 7, 8). Above all, the parallel between the question to Mary (20:15b: "Whom are you looking for?") and that to his first two disciples (1:38: "What are you looking for?") strictly binds the meaning of the verb to the discipleship situation. It qualifies as a search: of the Messiah announced by the Baptist, in the first case; of the Risen Christ, in the second. We can suppose, moreover, that the Johannine community was aware of the technical meaning of this "search," which involves commitment in view of the knowledge of the divine mysteries.[23]

Even more explicitly, then, Mary is recognized as a disciple based on the singular and intimate relationship that the Teacher establishes with her by calling her by name (20:16). Raymond E. Brown aptly sees here an explicit reference to the saying of the Good Shepherd (10:3b: "He calls his own sheep by name"), and Mary Magdalene was to serve as an example to present the new spiritual knowledge that is established between the Teacher and the disciples.[24] Nor should it be forgotten that in the Johannine tradition the intimacy of knowledge between disciple and teacher is always connected to the "orthodoxy" of the christological knowledge (see John 10:3–5; 1 John 2:4). If, for John, Mary of Magdala is the recipient of the first apparition of the Risen Lord, this fact necessarily has a precise Christian and ecclesiological implication.

The will on the part of Mary to ἄπτω (v. 17: "hold on to") Jesus, that is, to anchor the post-Easter knowledge of him to the already-experienced phase of his earthly life, is then doubly illuminating. It refers, on the one hand, to a historical experience of close contiguity, that is, to the already-lived experience of Mary as the Galilean disciple and her earthly knowledge of the Teacher. From the point of view of the literary construction, on the other hand, this term is also the dialectical element that allows one to arrive at the revelation of the full meaning of the resurrection and therefore to a new type of knowledge.

Starting from this passage from one to another type of knowledge, Mary will be invested by the Risen One himself with the role of announcing to the disciples the entirely new quality of the relationship that the exaltation of Jesus has established both between the Risen One and his disciples and between the disciples among themselves. Even the verb ἀγγέλλω (v. 18: to "announce") has a strong characterization, and the announcement of Mary commits the disciples in the renewal of the knowledge about Jesus; that is, it establishes the passage from the discipleship of the earthly Jesus to that of the Risen One. For John, the culmination of the ascension path, which in Luke corresponds to the intermediate time between resurrection and ascension, and which, for both, culminates in the outpouring of the Spirit (Luke 24:49a; John 20:22), is revealed to Mary during the Easter protophany, that is, the inclusion in God of Jesus, the Son, and of the disciples, who have now become ἀδελφούς (v. 17: "brothers") in the only Father. Significantly, it is the only time in John that the term *brothers* is used, except in 21:23, in which he explicitly means the community "of the disciple whom Jesus loved."

The ecclesial significance of this text is therefore very strong: on the christological foundation of faith in the resurrection, the continuity between the pre-Easter discipleship and the post-Easter discipleship of Mary of Magdala is asserted, and, at the same time, the role of this woman in guaranteeing the same continuity to the group of disciples through the passage from historical knowledge to the knowledge of the faith is attested. It is her testimony that opens the community to the appearance of the Risen One and to the outpouring of the Spirit (20:19–23).

The Theological Role of the Women in the Fourth Gospel

What has been said so far is reinforced by the fact that throughout the Fourth Gospel the theological role of the women is emphasized. Even leaving aside the story of the woman caught in adultery (7:53—8:11), because it is considered by many a non-Johannine later addition, the attention to the women who believe in Jesus from the tradition becomes evident, headed by the "disciple whom Jesus loved."[25] This attention is strongly characterized in a theological sense: like the Samaritan woman (4:5–42) and Martha (11:17–27), Mary of Magdala also intervenes dialectically in the development of a decisive doctrinal revelation on the part of Jesus.

According to Arianna Rotondo,[26] for John what matters is not so much a kind of rehabilitation of femininity, long discriminated, as instead a universal existential perspective, beyond gender, because at the center there is the word and not the sexuality of those who read it. From the point of view of a universal symbolic perspective, this is quite plausible, in my opinion. But, if seen in a historical perspective, things change, and the question becomes why a certain community prefers the protagonism of female figures and confers on them such a decisive theological function. There is no doubt that in the Gospel of John the symbolic dimension is of great importance. The problem of the interpretation of the symbols, however, is very serious because it can refer to either ideas, concepts, and figures in some way universal, to very specific and concrete realities to which is attributed paradigmatic value.

In the story of the Samaritan woman, the link between christological revelation and the opening of the apostolic mission to Samaria is revealed in Jesus's crucial statement on the overcoming of the traditional religious economy in the name of the worship of the Father in "spirit and truth" (4:24). The dialogue with Martha involves a crescendo on the part of this female disciple in the understanding of the doctrine of the resurrection, and culminates in the most important confession of faith in the Fourth Gospel, thus conferring upon the disciple of Bethany a role analogous to that acknowledged to Peter by virtue of his confession in Caesarea of Philippi (Mark 8:29; Matt 16:16; Luke 9:20). Martha's confession, however, finds its full meaning precisely in relation to the story of the Easter protophany to Mary of Magdala, of which it is the direct literary antecedent as well as the binding theological premise. The two episodes are connected by the thread of the theological elaboration of faith in the resurrection, that is, the identity nucleus of the emerging Christianity.

Similarly, in the story of the apparition on Easter morning, Mary of Magdala receives the revelation of the new state of life of the Risen One and can announce to the other disciples that she has seen, not Jesus or the Teacher, but τὸν κύριον (20:18: "the Lord"). The interlocutory claim of these three women effectively contributes, in short, to the passage from an uncertain and imprecise faith knowledge to the revelation of the mysteries of God. It is exactly this, in the Fourth Gospel, the theological characteristic of the faith-knowledge relationship.

Even the fourth woman to whom John gives critical importance, Mary of Bethany, provides an interesting parallel to Mary of Magdala, the female disciple who "seeks": in fact, Jesus himself openly defends her precisely at the beginning of the story of the passion and exactly in a controversy over discipleship (12:1–8).[27]

For the Fourth Evangelist, Martha's sister performs a symbolic embalming of Jesus. But one of the peculiarities of the Johannine account compared to the Synoptic ones is to present the contrast between Mary and Judas as a contraposition of types of discipleship. In John there is no opposition between an anonymous woman and anonymous guests, as in Mark and Matthew, or an anonymous "sinner" and a Pharisee, as in Luke, but two precise disciples, both called by name: Judas and Mary. Judas, moreover, is precisely identified as one of "his disciples": it is a dispute over the discipleship that the story intends to address.

Mary's gesture to pour oil to perfume Jesus's feet and to dry his feet with her hair is unusual because it is without biblical parallels, except for the Lucan tale of the sinful woman (see 7:38). It can only be interpreted within a symbolic horizon. In its quality of gestural prophecy,[28] it represents the recognition of Jesus as a temple, that is, as a visible sign of the presence of the God of Israel. Are we in a position to go back to the word of Jesus to the Samaritan woman and believe that the Johannine Christian women have contributed decisively to shift the axis of the identity of faith from the temple to the person of Jesus, the Christ of God? Everything seems to lead in this direction.

Here, too, as in the story of the Samaritan, the "woman" appears as a precise symbolic reference for the passage from the old to the new cult, from the old to the new temple, from the old to the new *ecclesia*. Within the Johannine communities, in which the presence and part of women played a major role, this is quite understandable. Precisely their presence and their role likely were nothing but a sign of this change and of its real effectiveness.

John does not, however, mention Jesus's praise of the woman of Bethany, which is, instead, the culmination of the Marcan story of the anointing because it confers an apostolic character on her prophetic gesture. John retains the reason for Jesus's legitimization of Mary's prophetic gesture, but does not define it, as Mark does, as "a good service." For him, the accent falls rather on the anticipatory force of the woman's gesture, a gesture that puts her in opposition to the disciple. The context of the word is not in question, as for the Samaritan woman, Martha, or Mary of Magdala, so much so that even in John, as in the other versions of the story, the woman does not even say a word. In her prophecy of gestures, the emphasis falls on the fact that Jesus takes a strong position, silencing the disciple and confirming the woman in her action.

"Leave her alone": this is how the story ends. The discipleship of the woman is therefore confirmed: Jesus recognizes the prophetic character expressed in her symbolic action. Does the story contain any trace of the presence, even within the Johannine church, of that tendency, typically institutional, hostile to prophecy, often embodied instead by women? It is difficult to reach such a conclusion with certainty. No doubt, it attests to the will of the evangelist to support the prophetic ministry, attributing it to Mary of Bethany, one of those whom Jesus loved (see 11:5), and defending her from the attacks of "one of his disciples" (12:4).

The fact that the memory of these three female disciples was preserved in the Johannine communities and, even more so, the use of this memory by the evangelist show a clear recognition within the Johannine tradition of the participation of the women both in the evangelization and the development of the doctrinal elaboration. The context of the word, far from being precluded to them, is exactly where their vigorous subjectivity is openly attested. They are not only full-fledged disciples, they are also fully involved in the doctrinal elaboration that will make the Johannine text the most theologically developed Gospel.

A final note on an apparently marginal element that, in addition to reinforcing what has been said so far, raises an important question: in the story of the Easter apparition to Mary of Magdala, the angels first and then Jesus himself address the disciple with the title of "woman" (20:13, 15). It is a fact that, in the Fourth Gospel, the "woman" title in the mouth of Jesus occurs more frequently than in the Synoptics, above all in contexts of pronounced christological importance: we have seen that Jesus uses it twice to address his mother, at Cana (2:4) and on the cross (19:26), as well as to the Samaritan woman (4:21). In all these cases, there is something important at stake regarding the revelation about Jesus. Ambrose had already noted it, giving it an interpretation that deserves to be remembered because it is a small lesson in traditional gender theology: Jesus calls her "woman" because he still considers her according to the quality of her physical sex, for she who believes arrives "to maturity, to the measure of the full stature of Christ" (Eph 4:13).[29]

It seems to me quite legitimate, at least, to ask ourselves whether the recurrence of this title in the Fourth Gospel cannot refer to a gender subjectivity that concerns not only the singularity of individual figures, albeit paradigmatic and exemplary. Perhaps, in the communities that had assimilated the tradition of the "disciple whom Jesus loved," the presence of women was particularly relevant and their contribution to the theological elaboration of the tradition received was particularly active. The attribution to them of actions such as ζητέω, λαλέω, κηρύσσω (seek, speak, announce) offers, in this regard, a precise testimony and therefore clearly refers to prominent figures of the Johannine school.

Apostle of the Risen Christ

Finally, in John's account Mary of Magdala does not need an intermediate time to dissolve doubts and uncertainties: the passage from angelophany to Christophany is almost immediate and, for her, an announcement of the resurrection through the sign given by the angels and the apparition of the Risen One coincide. From here, then, Christ's apostolic mandate springs forth, the first after his resurrection.

The very significant element of the uncertainty and perplexity that also occurs, as we saw earlier, in the Synoptics, is recovered with the insertion of the passage that narrates the testimony of Mary to the disciples regarding the empty tomb; and the race of Peter and the "other disciple…toward the tomb" (20:2–10) is a very significant element in this regard, that of the competition between the two disciples.[30] For them, the tomb is not a place of prophetic announcement and only in part is a place of revelation. True, John says, "The other disciple…saw and believed," but immediately after he also states that—and this is one of the many inconsistencies of the Johannine text—"for as yet they did not understand the scripture, that he must rise from the dead" (v. 9).

This is a point that deserves some consideration. What must have happened in the disciples and among the disciples in the hours and days immediately after Jesus's death is difficult to know. The clues that come to us from the Gospel narratives are very few and, above all, indirect. Certainly, it must have taken some time for the groups of believers in Jesus to find convincing words to express faith in the resurrection—a time when charismatic testimonies of faith in the resurrection must have been intertwined together and, as John says, there was an investigation of the Scriptures to trace elements of continuity between the Jewish expectation of the Son of Man and the Nazarene, the Crucified and Resurrected. A time when, in the context of the Pauline mission, the distinctly soteriological dimension of Christology developed instead.

For John, everything is concentrated in the Risen One's word "I am ascending to my Father and your Father, to my God and your God" (20:17), and the Magdalene's ability not to bind herself to the memory of the dead Teacher, to not want "to hold on," but to accept his new pneumatic dimension. How long it lasted and what led to this passage or, to put it in Jesus's words of promise to the disciples before delivering himself to death, what it entailed to enter the dimension of the Spirit (14:25–26; 15:26–27; 16:12ff.), we do not know.

Of course, in any of its forms, faith in the resurrection has always had a propulsive dimension. From the angelic mission to the women to prepare the disciples for the encounter with the Risen Lord in Galilee (Mark 16:7), to the solemn missionary mandate in Matthew (28:16ff.), to the mission announced by Luke (24:49) and presented at the beginning of the Book of Acts (1:6–8), to the vocation of Paul (Gal 1:15–16): each apparition of the Risen One creates an apostolic sending. The same applies to Mary of Magdala. In a strictly communitarian sense, so much suggests that the Johannine community must have been indebted to her for the genesis of its faith in the resurrection and its own apostolic foundation.

From the earliest times, the Western tradition has wished to give her the title of "apostle of the apostles," relaunched today, in times of feminism, with great emphasis. It may seem paradoxical, but it is an equivocal expression. At the end of his report to the Plenary Assembly of the German Conference of Bishops entitled *The Collaboration of Men and Women in the Church and in the World,* held in Trier on February 23, 2000, Cardinal Walter Kasper came to wish, "Perhaps today we are in need again of an *apostola apostolorum* like Mary of Magdala, who on Easter morning awakened the apostles from their lethargy and set them in motion."[31] It might seem not only a desire but a promising hope for the future of the Church. However, some of Kasper's statements made earlier suggest that, for Mary of Magdala, the title of *apostola apostolorum* is too often used only as a rhetorical expression. In fact, according to Kasper, "regarding the presbyterate in particular, it is not a matter of the equal dignity of all Christians" because the salvific mediation is only possible *in persona Christi* and "the real-symbolic *repraesentatio Christi* as the spouse of his bride, who is the Church, according to the concordant tradition of the Churches of the East and of the West, in the biblical symbolism pertaining to sexuality is masculine." John Paul II expresses the same opinion in the apostolic letter *Ordinatio Sacerdotalis.*[32]

Apart from the fact that the sexual symbolism applied to the relationship Christ-Church should be handled with greater care, the crucial question is another: Why in the ecclesiastical lexicon the title "Prince of the Apostles" attributed to Peter and his successors has had, and has, a tremendous importance, even though it does not derive from the language of the New Testament and in fact contradicts its meaning, whereas the title "apostle of the apostles" can be so easily emptied of ecclesial value? Is Mary an apostle or not? And if she is an apostle, does she enter the apostolic succession at least like Paul? Obviously, it is not a matter of slipping into nominalism.

The Eastern tradition acknowledges to Mary the title of ἰσαπόστολος (equal to the apostles), but from a ministerial point of view, this equality has never had the necessary repercussions. However, it is a question of explaining the semantic shifts that are attributed to words that, from the theological point of view, have an indisputable relevance.

The reflection on John's text of the first apparition of the Risen One should then be more attentive. In fact, the evangelist does not love the title of apostles,[33] and Mary is rather sent to the "brothers," that is, to all the disciples. Perhaps, sooner or later, finally, we will come to recognize that the title due to her is "apostle of Christ." It is Jesus who orders the disciple-who-seeks to go and announce to the brothers that he has now returned to the Father where he had come from (see 13:1). Paul had to fight to obtain the title of ἀπόστολος τοῦ Χριστου (apostle of Christ). Mary probably had to do the same.

Chapter 5

Transition

But not having the strength to preach, for her sex was too frail for such a task, it was to men that the duty of preaching was entrusted.

Ambrose, *Exposition of the Gospel of Luke*[1]

I attend a funeral. The celebrant gives in to liturgical rhetoric, a little too emphatic in gesture as in word, perhaps due to his youth. What strikes me is his biblical ignorance. He rightly incites those present to remain steadfast in the faith by calling as witnesses the figures painted along the nave of the church. "These are the apostles," he says, "weak men [*sic!*] who abandoned Jesus on the eve of his death." I look up: among the strictly male figures there are also Paul and Matthias who, of course, were not with Jesus in the days following his resurrection. This at least he should know.

As for the rest, I think of the fact that the theological formation of that young priest is still affected by "anthropocentric bias" that weighs like a boulder on our exegesis and theology, but no less on our iconographic tradition. Paradoxically, I sometimes wonder if it would be better if our churches, with all their wealth of images, disappeared and then were rebuilt as the fruit of a theological culture that has finally rendered justice to the truth of the facts. After all—and it should not be so irrelevant—among these "facts" there is the story of Jesus of Nazareth, his male and female disciples, his male and female apostles. It is a plural story.

A plural story because it is inhabited by men and women, but also plural because it is the result of the separation and intertwining of so many different traditions. The story of Jesus, the Galilean who recognized himself in John the Baptist's movement rather than in other official or marginal groups of his time, intersects that

89

of other Israelites, that of his disciples with that of other sons of Abraham, men and women who lived in Palestine of the first century during the Roman occupation. History is always plural, and every monochromatic reduction of its colors alters and betrays it. But historiography, as we know, has been, and is very often in black and white.

The history of the post-Easter movement is also plural—at least until the rise and supremacy of a majoritarian and more powerful current that did not erase the traces of the history of other groups who believed in the Risen One and did not raise a border between canonical and apocryphal, between who was in and who was out, between orthodoxy and heresy. Only from the moment in which, after centuries, scholars of both camps have begun to cross this border in one sense or another, almost to the point of eroding it, it became finally clear that on that borderline it was possible to discover the traces of the women who believed in Jesus as Messiah and Risen One. Figures exiled from the canonical memory, forced out of the great Church, branded as belonging to heretical movements.

Among them, at the center, once again, we find Mary of Magdala, confirming a discipleship and apostolic primacy that could not but create tradition: in the "apocryphal" territories remain traces of an apostolic genealogy that is led by the Galilean woman who had followed Jesus from Galilee to Jerusalem, who shared with him the proclamation of the kingdom, who received from him, once he rose again, the apostolic investiture.

It is therefore necessary to enter the "apocryphal" territories because the canonical memory is affected by anthropocentric bias. In the marginal circles of ancient Christianity, the interest in Mary of Magdala has instead grown by means of various kinds of thrusts. According to François Bovon, this interest may have been caused by influences of either the mythological narratives of pagan origin, in which Jesus and Mary would correspond to a Christian rendering of mythical couples, or the Hellenistic novel that took, above all, the form of romance novels. More credible, in my opinion, is the third, more sociological hypothesis presented by the French scholar, according to which the importance of Mary Magdalene is due to the claims of the women of some Christian sects of the second century. In this case, the jealousy of the apostles would express, symmetrically, the resistance of both the men of these groups and that of the great Church to this feminine claim.[2]

A few centuries later, Ambrose will rationalize what happened: if the one who had first received the apostolic mandate from Christ himself has disappeared from the missionary horizon, this can only be because of her own inadequacy, better yet, the inadequacy of her sex: "But not having the strength to preach, for her sex was too frail for such a task, it was to men that the duty of preaching was entrusted."[3] And so, the exclusion of women from the apostolic succession is accomplished: as evidenced by the history behind us, and the one still in place in many countries of the world today, for the patriarchy the *impedimentum sexus* is all-encompassing and does not concern only the cultic sphere.

Peter was evangelized by Mary, not the other way around. Yet, Peter became the prince of the apostles. To Mary Magdalene, now out of the process of authoritative transmission of the faith, all that is left is the honor of the legend, which seems never ending since it is able to nourish itself with always new esoteric elements: the forgiven sinner of the great ecclesiastical tradition becomes the mother of Jesus's children and her descendants spread all over Europe through the various ruling houses. Strange fate indeed is that of Mary of Magdala: mother of kings and queens in the thousand streams of local traditions, popular legends, and literary fantasies; the important thing is that, in no way, an apostolic genealogy is to be ascribed to her.

Between the two parts of this study there are considerable differences, due primarily to the chronology and typology of the writings examined: in the following section, the historical features of Mary of Magdala, emerging from the pages of the Gospels, pass the baton to another genre of historicity, that of the communities, of women and men, who in the following centuries referred to Mary Magdalene.

The survey of the entire ancient Christian literature, which would include what in theological studies is still called patristic, would have expanded in a disproportionate and perhaps even ineffective manner the second part of this book, which focuses rather on writings that have a claim to authority but were not welcomed into the canon of the great Church, or originated already outside or in contraposition to its incipient constitution. They are generally called apocryphal and what remains often *hidden* is the concrete situation that produced, preserved, and used them. The presentation that is offered here does not aim to be exhaustive, due also to the variety and complexity that characterizes this literature, but rather aims to unearth the models of the *genealogy* of Mary. From the past to the present, personal and communal dimensions, roles once acted and spiritualities once lived, were shaped and dealt with her memory.

All this inevitably passes through the reality of women and men and the imagery of the *masculine* and *feminine*, in their concrete interaction. Therefore, it concerns us: as the ancients wanted it to be, since everyone, man and woman, becomes the protagonist of the narration, or as the lesson of the last century wants it to be, because history is always contemporary, and therefore implicating and transformative.

PART II

AN APOSTLE BETWEEN SPIRITUALITY AND CONFLICT

❧ The Apocryphal Tradition ❧

CRISTINA SIMONELLI

Chapter 6

A Framework of Reference

To sharply separate Christian writings into canonical, edifying/ doctrinal—that is, patristic—and apocryphal cannot but be dictated by apologetic or marketing reasons. The distinction, however, if it maintains flexibility, has some validity, even of a historical nature: ancient and modern classifications are still a way of expressing convictions by organizing the data. The parameters thus formed respond to different criteria, some internal to the writings themselves, but many of them external, linked to the prevailing attitude of those who created them. The materials can also be arranged differently, and this is even more evident when the operation is linked to legitimization or, to the contrary, of exclusion from power, whatever that may be. It is understandable therefore that to follow the feminine traces—that is, of women, of the narratives that concern them, of the characteristics attributed to them—allows to have renewed parameters, which also shed new light on the historical reconstruction.

APOCRYPHAL LITERATURE, APOCRYPHAL HISTORY

Apocryphal etymologically means "hidden." The term, already known in the classical period, assumes a particular meaning in the Christian era and is used with a negative connotation as early as the second century of the current era by authors such as Irenaeus of Smyrna/Lyon, who uses it to oppose a tradition that is in some way public, available for anyone, to the secret traditions that only individual teachers can communicate to their disciples. In the Alexandrian environment, more prone to esoteric spiritual models, the term sounds less negative.

At the same time, there were some early lists of the "canon" proper—like the late second-century *Muratorian Fragment*—that after the works were accepted and compiled by the Church, present at the bottom some disputable or rejected texts. The terms used for the latter vary, but at some point—for example, in the fifth century of the Latin language—they are called *apocrypha*, which remains broad, so that in the *Gelasian Decree* it includes any text considered not in conformity with that officially accepted. The stakes at play are those of the collective memory, recognized and "authorized" of Jesus of Nazareth, which is thus linked to a unitary plexus: certain convictions, certain texts, certain people. Among the latter, at a very early stage, a distinction is drawn between the primary witnesses, who can claim a direct knowledge or in any case an extremely close one, as it was mediated by a small number of people, and those who in the following ages can transmit the entirety of these traditions.

The writings that today are called *apocryphal* are not part of the first section of the official lists; at most, they appear in some cases in the section of the writings discussed or in any case not to be read publicly. They are not the only ones, however, because they share this same condition with other texts, commonly classified according to Catholic confessional terminology, like *patristic*, or according to Jean B. Cotelier's (1672) expression, even *Apostolic Fathers*. One of these, for example, is the Roman *Shepherd of Hermas*, a book composed of prophetic/apocalyptic visions highly esteemed in the community of the capital of the empire. It is mentioned at the foot of the *Muratorian Fragment* in the following terms:

> But Hermas wrote The Shepherd very recently, in our times, in the city of Rome, while bishop Pius, his brother, was occupying the chair of the church of the city of Rome. And therefore it ought indeed to be read, but it cannot be read publicly to the people of the church either among the prophets, whose number is complete, or among the apostles, for it is after [their] time.

In this context, a phenomenon is soon evident and easily understandable: only the interpretation of the writings accepted in the canon is free, and in some contexts such as the Alexandrian one, this gives rise to explanations and multiple interpretive levels, while the texts as such are protected and forbidden, with variants of no great significance. For the other writings instead, the opposite phenomenon becomes evident: they are written and rewritten with much greater freedom, thus giving rise to very wide combinations and variants. For this reason, apocryphal literature is a vast and complex world, with varying and shifting texts, which extend for a vast chronological period, often encrypted by pseudo-epigraphic backdating because the writings *must* be traced back to figures of the first Christian generation.

Among the features that distinguish them is the claim of authenticity/authoritativeness, achieved through the attribution of the writing to an already known and important name in the circle of the first witnesses: Thomas, John, Philip, Mary, Barnabas, James brother of Jesus, Paul. This procedure is evident at a first reading and, in most cases, it develops through a consistent intertextuality, a kind of *remake* of otherwise known writings. In fact, they often appear as extensions, discussions, and critiques of an earlier text, both Jewish and Christian: this is what happens, for example, in the *Gospel of the Birth of Mary* (= the mother of Jesus), which contains a *typical* sequence (birth of Mary, her life, birth of Jesus, flight into Egypt) attributed to the memories of James, son of Joseph and therefore brother of Jesus, the eyewitness of those events. For this reason, Guillaume Postel proposed to publish it (1549–50) with the title of *Protoevangelium of James*.

The text presents countless elements of the narratives of the "canonical gospels of Matthew and Luke" and many Old Testament themes: for instance, the *exodal* image of the cloud that accompanies the divine manifestation, or the immobility of the world at the birth of Jesus, very similar to Joshua's words "Sun, stand still." Their modern and contemporary classification is based on recognizable criteria, but the inclusion or exclusion of some texts still depends on the point of view of those who propose the parameters and publish the collections, like the work of the compilers of the ancient lists. The modern conception of apocrypha within biblical sciences begins with the work of J. A. Fabricius, who published a collection of writings in two volumes (1703–19), titled *Codex apocryphus Novi*

Testamenti and *Codex pseudepigraphus Veteris Testamenti.* Since 1987, an international group of scholars (AELAC)[1] has used the term "Christian apocryphal literature," which is quite widespread despite the previous diversified confessional use: in the Protestant context, apocrypha are those writings that the Catholic and Orthodox Church have accepted in their canon but are not in the Hebrew—the "deuterocanonical" in Catholic terminology—while the Jewish writings not present in any of the canonical collections, the same ones that are elsewhere referred to as intertestamental, are called "pseudoepigrapha."

As already noted, however, the parameters used by researchers affect the lists, which in turn determine the diffusion of some texts more than others. Regarding Mary Magdalene, this process takes on a significant meaning because it directs the reception, confining her memory to specific contexts, be they feminist studies, spiritual interpretation,[2] or "archaic-gossip" as seen with Dan Brown. For example, we can observe that two writings on which we will focus, particularly the *Gospel of Mary* and the *Pistis Sophia,* well known to Luigi Moraldi, are collected in a compact format under the title of *Vangeli Gnostici* and in an edition reserved to the *Pistis Sophia,* but not within the collection of *Vangeli Apocrifi* he edited for Piemme editions (1996). However, the same scholar has included the *Pistis Sophia* among the ten texts published in the collection titled *Testi gnostici* (UTET 1982) in which it is the only text that is not part of the Nag Hammadi collection. The absence of the *Gospel of Mary* is noticeable again in the *I Vangeli apocrifi,* edited by Marcello Craveri for Einaudi (1969, re-edited in 1990), or in the collection for Giunti (1994, updated in 2016), edited by Angela Cerinotti. Mario Erbetta instead has generously included both writings in his extensive collection (Marietti 1966, three volumes: *Vangeli, Atti e Leggende, Lettere e Apocalissi*).

In the classification, the chronological period within which the collection is to be kept is also relevant: most of the authors limit the study to ancient texts, that is, contemporary to the great patristic tradition of the fourth and fifth centuries, given the very mobile status of codices and their variants, however within the first millennium, while others include contemporary ones.

Perceptive, in this regard, are Pierluigi Piovanelli's comments regarding "an apocryphal hermeneutic," in which he points out and comments on the choices underlying the largest contemporary collections (Hennecke and Schneemelcher for the German-speaking area, the Plèiade edition, the result of the AELAC in French) with respect to the inclusion or not of later texts. Piovanelli suggests taking into consideration contemporary works as well because they are all the result of a same process of self-narration through the reconstruction of the origins.[3]

In any case, the historical and critical attention that has characterized the twentieth century prevents us from being satisfied with a single reconstruction of the past, whatever it may be. It is suspicious of official reconstructions, linked to groups of power that somehow got the spotlight. In this horizon, there have been widespread uses of different "apocrypha," which retain the meaning of hidden and inauthentic, but attribute and distribute them differently. In the first case, *apocryphal* can refer to the subjects and processes hidden in the official tradition, and with this meaning the theologian Ivana Ceresa claims to look for *apocryphal women*, that is, the ones removed, suppressed in history, but whose traces can and must be recovered. In the second meaning, Maria Zambrano inverts the question: using apocryphal in the sense of inauthentic, she maintains that apocryphal is the official story that leaves out important people and events: "it is the apocryphal story—not for this reason less certain—that covers the true one. Because, yes, the apocryphal story almost always suffocates the true one, the story that philosophical reason is anxious to reveal and establish and the poetic reason is anxious to redeem."[4] Emblematic is a passage from one of her books *Delirium and Destiny*, in which an innkeeper states, "This is the disgrace that befalls us who live in such poor and isolated countries, sir, Mr. tax collector, or whatever is the name of His grace: these things happen and then there is never someone who can tell them!"[5] Similarly, Mary Daly distinguishes between a mystifying front stage and what really matters, that the close-ups conceal, whose existence has no robust documentary evidence, but whose absence does not *simply* coincide with nonexistence.[6]

Our reading is at the intersection of these coordinates: it deals with "Christian apocryphal" texts but does not see them only as excluded from the biblical canon. Rather, it values them as traces of situations, people, roles that have been concealed; their renewed reading renders any reconstruction of Christian antiquity that does not include them, if not inauthentic, at least partially so.

APOSTOLIC *GENEALOGIES*

In the process just described, starting from the second century, ideas, writings, and guarantors form a unitary plexus; we will focus on the guarantors and on the authoritative genealogies that refer to them.

The work of Papias of Hierapolis, of whose five books some fragments remain, is an example of what Enrico Norelli, following Jan Assman, repeatedly calls the transition from an affective memory to a cultural one. In the foreground are the direct witnesses in an oral sequence, but their memories are written down. In Irenaeus, who is a witness but also the one who compiles and disseminates an important tradition in this regard, this process forms the idea of apostolicity. In this sense, this is a very serious issue, as it also includes a group of public writings and basic beliefs and only within this paradigm are inserted figures that guarantee its continuity. Since, however, these men are considered in "apostolic succession," the system also contributes to establishing an idea of apostles that was at once very narrow and, at the same time, dangerously extended. In fact, as far as origins are concerned, it is reductive as it confirms the identity between "twelve" and "apostles," which is not at all common in the "canonical" texts.[7] However, it becomes extremely loose with regard to subsequent epochs: although it does not dare to call "apostles" those who preside over the churches (bishops/presbyters in the still-unstable terminology present in Irenaeus), it places them "in the apostolic succession" and thus helps to bind the group that exercises authority to authorized genealogies and vice versa.

Already in the writings accepted in the same period in the canon, the names and qualifications of the people form uneven maps: among these are the Twelve, called apostles mainly in Luke's work, and there is the emblematic case of Paul, who in no way corresponds to the criteria offered in Acts 1:21–22. Then there are other names, present in various ways in the writings: Nicodemus and James the brother of Jesus, and "all" the women: Martha and Mary of Bethany, Mary Magdalene, Mary the Mother of Jesus, Mary of Cleophas. Of the Gospels accepted in the churches as canonical, only Matthew is directly linked to the name of one of the Twelve, of which neither Mark nor Luke are part, while it is the tradition that consistently links the Fourth Gospel to John.

If in the texts we find the echo of diversified practices, the interpretation that is mainly made of them is further biased and selective: suffice it here to observe a prominent figure such as that of Cephas/Peter. From ancient times to the present, especially in the West and in the Catholic version, the passages that are highlighted are the ones stressing his role—the confession of Mark 8:29 and especially Matthew 16:16–18, or the precedence in the apparition of the Risen One in Luke 24:34—while are left in the background the passages in which he appears as the one who does not understand, who has little faith, or even denies Jesus. In fact, these are read at most in an edifying key, to show his capacity for repentance and have no bearing on the role established in relation to him in the churches that refer to them in a particular way, Rome among them all. The process is exactly the opposite of what happens to Martha or Mary of Magdala: everything that concerns them leaves the level of institution and authority and becomes a moral, spiritual, or symbolic fact.

Peter and Mary Magdalene represent the two extreme poles of the parable and are often opposed also in the texts we will examine in this section, but the same process can also be found for other figures: the conflicts that emerge around the three so-called pillars (Cephas; James, the brother of Jesus; and John: Gal 2:9 in the Pauline letters) and those who have important roles in Acts (James, Peter in Acts 15), or the figure of the beloved disciple and his Johannine legacy right into the heart of the second-century debate on the celebration of Easter[8] are examples of how some traditions relate to a person, which then becomes the eponym of an authorizing genealogy and its specific *marker*.

In this sense, another typical case is that of Thomas called Didymus; his role in the Fourth Gospel represents a junction of some relevance, which in the West resonates with the reproach to those who cannot trust the chain of witnesses. But an insightful Syro-Mesopotamian tradition remembers him as the evangelizer of those regions and makes of his appellation "Didymus" the sign of an unheard proximity to Jesus: he would be Jesus's twin through his request for greater closeness to the mystery of the resurrection. Even the churches of India, particularly of Kerala, consider him their evangelizer, calling themselves Thomas Christians: Latinized by the missionaries of Francis Xavier, today they come together in the Syrian Malabar and Syrian Malagasy rites. This Eastern tradition, which also boasts of burials and other archaeological finds, has produced a large literary cycle, a corpus attributed to Thomas, which goes from the collection of *loghia* largely parallel to the Synoptic ones contained in the *Gospel of Thomas*, the *Acts of Thomas*, and an Arabic *Infancy Gospel*, all in connection with the *Acts of Addai* (Thaddeus). These are part of the writings not accepted in the canon, therefore they are apocryphal in the modern meaning of the term, and in the state in which they can be read today, they present different dualistic elements, consisting in their distrust verging on contempt for materiality and especially for sexuality. What is practically impossible to decipher is whether the collections that include them have these characteristics because they originated this way or have integrated them because the writings have become almost exclusive property of groups that had such convictions.

Even Peter's figure is not exempt from such a process: in the canonical collection the First and Second Letter of Peter are attributed to him in pseudo-epigraphic form, and Papia recognizes the ideological paternity of Mark's Gospel in him. He is also the protagonist of a large apocryphal collection (*Gospel of Peter, Acts of Peter, Pseudo-Clementine Writings*) that links him to Rome through various episodes, including the famous *Quo vadis?* anecdote confirming it, just like the Christians of India, even with the presence of burials. Besides, the "tombs" are also important in the aforementioned Easter question: Polycrates of Ephesus replies to Victor of Rome, who probably boasted about the burials of Peter and Paul in

Rome, that if tombs serve to support a tradition, in Asia there are many: John at Ephesus, Melito of Sardis, Polycarp and the daughters of Philip (Eusebius, *Ecclesiastical History* V, 23–25). Burials as a site of devotion in the fourth century show a still wide apostolic map: the pilgrim Egeria during her travels will visit the tombs of Thomas in Edessa, John in Ephesus, and of Thecla in Seleucia.

In this case, however, the church of Rome, oblivious to the fact that the canonical corpus does not record Cephas's presence in the city, has fully accepted the tradition of the apocryphal Acts. The same church also refers to the memory of Paul, whose presence in Rome (Acts and Epistle to Romans) is much more firmly documented. But if in the fifth century Pope Leo, in contrast to the Canon of Chalcedon XXIII, advances the inclusive Petrine-Pauline apostolic memory as the place of authorization of that church, in the Latin third century there had already been a clear prevailing of the Roman memory of Peter over that of Paul.

As for the female characters, similar dynamics are evident, but with some peculiar characteristics. On the one hand, there are the women mentioned in the "canonical" writings. Besides Mary, the mother of Jesus, Martha and Mary of Bethany, and Mary Magdalene have a prominent place: in antiquity, to Martha are not attributed specific genealogies, despite the importance of her figure and her profession of faith; Mary Magdalene, with her prominent role in relation the Risen One, gives rise to a specific literature that, however, remains predominantly confined to certain contexts, while in other writings, dynamically crosscutting different languages and contexts, she is replaced, with the complicity of homonymy, by Mary, the mother of Jesus. John Paul II based a meditation on these writings, which aroused amazement and confusion.

However, before addressing the ones regarding Mary Magdalene, we must at least remember two complementary and, in some sense, specular data: the poor fortune of women mentioned in canonical writings and the creation of traditions on other women who are not named in them. As for the former, according to the surviving testimonies, there is not a genealogy of Priscilla with her husband Aquila nor of Junia with Andronicus; the same goes for Phoebe *diakonos* of the church of Cenchrea in Corinth, who, for example, enters in the typology of female diaconal figures only in the *Barberini Euchologion* (seventh century), while she is absent in the ordination rite of the deaconesses in the fourth-century *Apostolic Constitutions*. The opposite happens to Thecla, the female protagonist of the *Acts of Paul*, which in many manuscripts is referred to as *Acts of Paul and Thecla*.

A text by Tertullian written in Carthage in the very first years of the third century is useful both to verify the dating and circulation of the text, which is thus placed at the end of the previous century, and to show how some Carthaginian women relied on the *authority* of Thecla to legitimize their *ministerial* action:

> But the forwardness [*petulantia*] of a woman who has presumed to teach [*quae usurpavit docere*] will not of course acquire for her the right of baptizing also, unless some new beast appear like unto the old, so that just as that one took away Baptism,[9] so some beast should by herself confer it. But if they claim writings which are wrongly inscribed with Paul's name—I mean the example of Thecla—in support of women's freedom to teach and baptize, let them know that a presbyter in Asia, who put together that book, heaping up a narrative as it were from his own materials under Paul's name, when after conviction he confessed that he had done it from love of Paul, resigned his position. (Tertullian, *On Baptism*, 17:4–5)

Egeria, who, as mentioned earlier, visits Thecla's tomb at Seleucia, also reports that in her memory there was a monastic community of men and women, presided over by the deaconess Martana, whom she herself had met during a visit to Jerusalem.

Perhaps the question is still intended to remain unanswered, but it is natural to wonder why Mary Magdalene does not seem to have had the same function: the women of Carthage who referred to Thecla would have found in Mary Magdalene an equally strong figure of evangelizer, which, at the present state of research, emerges only in the Greek *Acts of Philip* and then, in other respects, in some medieval revisitations.

But these questions, even if destined to remain so, are never futile. Moreover, in this case, they never rely on a single aspect, because they also include, among others, the question of the relationship between writing and orality, the problem of the nonhomogeneous dissemination of canonical writings, and of the reception of the Johannine work, as well as the gender dynamics involving notions of sexuality and role attributions.

In any case, from this point of view, reading the "apocryphal" cycles of Paul, Peter, John, Philip, and Thomas means not only studying an archaic literature, but it also means researching the events of the different communities that referred to them. Is there even *a church of Mary?* The writings we are dealing with here confirm it, even if their authorizing potential remains largely the preserve of marginalized groups, in which, paradoxically, the reference to female genealogies ends up rather reinforcing exclusion.

GNOSTICISM: THE LANGUAGE OF "ELSEWHERE"

To begin reading the apocryphal texts that deal in different ways with Mary Magdalene, it is worth recalling some coordinates of the Gnostic phenomenon, so that when the comment meets the term, we can refer to a plausible and shared conceptual map.

In fact, the term *gnôsis* means "knowledge" and is therefore much wider than the use that associates it with a religious and philosophical school that intersects the Christian phenomenon, especially between the second and third century. Its exploration is made complex by many reasons: the status of the sources, the esoteric language and the mythologizing taste of the well-known writings, the eclectic form of the themes that does not allow simplifying appropriations in one or another religious area, and finally the absence of a reality that connects the individual groups, so that the experience as such is hard to rebuild. In the studies of Christian antiquity, the reference to the boundaries indicated in the so-called Messina colloquium of 1966, which takes as the interpretive key the reality of the second century, reserving instead a broader and transversal sense to gnosis/Gnostics, as synonyms of spiritual paths in which prevails the cognitive element and the elitist trait:

To avoid an undifferentiated use of the terms *gnosis* and Gnosticism, it seems to be advisable to identify, by combined use of historical and typological methods, a concrete fact, "Gnosticism," beginning methodologically with a certain group of systems of the Second Century A.D. which everyone agrees are to be designated by this term. In distinction from this, *gnosis* is regarded as "knowledge of the divine mysteries reserved for an elite."[10]

Within such an area, there is a galaxy of groups linked to individual teachers but with some elements in common: in the face of Christian Gnostic movements, different dynamics are set in motion in other ecclesial communities, which, on the one hand, accept some speculations (e.g., on the Logos and trinitarian monotheism); on the other hand, they reject their fundamental traits such as radical dualism, with the resulting contempt of materiality and the esoteric form, often related to the revelations known only to the group's teacher. Overall, the question is not extraneous to the formation of the Christian canon and is often one of the contexts in which the dialogues of revelation of the Risen One develop, which are important in the writings we are dealing with here.

For a long time, the knowledge of the phenomenon has been dependent on the responses of the great Church to the "Gnostic" groups that professed themselves to be Christians and often represented true intellectual elites. This *antiheretical* literature consists of paraphrases of the Gnostic writings, from excerpts embedded in the answers, or from forceful pamphlets of accusation. In short, the criticisms focus on the method, which, as mentioned earlier, gives great importance to the doctrinal formulation of the single teacher, and the dualistic content that, if developed, gives rise to a very different development of Christianity from the one now known by that name.

A central *myth* also emerges from the whole, in which cosmogony is also a theogony. The world as it is experienced is the result of a divine problem, often identified in the transgression of the last of the divine polarities (aeons), Sophia, which breaks the intradivine order and, rejected outside, gives rise to an incomplete birth, that is, to a troubled world that, however, contains some divine spark. Salvation consists then in retracing that journey backward, bringing back the spark that the best find in themselves to the "whole of the divine" (= pleroma). However, there are also names (Valentine, Theodore, Heraklion, Basilides) and a sort of circulation map, which has a major pole in Alexandria in Egypt, but also affirms its presence in Rome and other places; otherwise, it would be difficult to understand the transversal nature of the responsiveness of figures of the second/third century as Irenaeus of Lyon (Gaul/ Rome), the author of the *Elenchos* (Rome), as well as the Alexandrian Clement and Origen.

As is understandable, between the nineteenth and twentieth centuries there was a certain lack of confidence in the possibility of knowing Gnosticism through this literature because the sources were all on the opposite party and therefore appeared unreliable. The status of the studies has changed considerably with the find in Egypt in 1945 of a whole collection of Coptic texts attributable to Gnosticism: the codices, all extremely refined, had been found in a sealed jar not far from al-Qasr, the ancient Chenoboskion, in one of the many caverns of the Jabal cliff in Tarif, in the same area where Pachomian monasticism flourished. The nearby town of Nag Hammadi has now lent its name to the entire collection. The thirteen large codices were copied between the fourth and fifth centuries, mostly translating originals in Greek or already in Greek translation, and contain some works dating back to the second century, including the so-called *Apocryphon of John*, considered by many a basic form of the theogonic model in question; the writing was already known also to Irenaeus of Lyon, who had paraphrased it. The substantial correctness of Irenaeus's reading has in part revalued the interpretation of the anti-Gnostic writings, which proved to be at least informed on the texts they intended to refute. However, what is still unclear—and it could not be otherwise—is the practical setting and the spiritual experience, which the writings hint at but in encrypted and esoteric form, thus leaving room for many conjectures.

No doubt, Nag Hammadi is more than just a collection of writings: a *library* presupposes a community that collects—perhaps the same one that is committed to translating—preserves and uses. We do not know at this moment "who" was behind it, how such practice was structured, and if it did so in an exclusive form, separated in the fifth century from other Christian and perhaps monastic forms. Nor can Gnosticism coincide with Nag Hammadi, in the sense that the news of the existence of Gnostics indicates a larger map, but there are no such large collections so conspicuously preserved in other places. Moreover, the writings collected in the Coptic language originated elsewhere, many in the same Greek-speaking Egypt of the second and third century, but others could come from the Syriac area, perhaps already arrived however through a Greek translation, like the *Gospel of Thomas* present in Codex II.

At the same time, some of the texts examined in the following chapters are, in a sense, parallel to the Nag Hammadi collection, but even though they came from Egypt, they were not part of that collection (or were separated before its discovery), a sign of a wider dissemination of the experience. One of these is *Pistis Sophia*, which among the various dimensions that characterize it, presents a strong protagonism of Mary of Magdala and a practical dimension, only sketchy, but not irrelevant: the spiritual path is marked by prayers, which follow one another and are interpreted one with the help of the other. The prayers are represented by hymns that are unique to the text, biblical Psalms and the *Odes of Solomon*, a Christian Syrian-Aramaic collection otherwise well attested. But the codex containing the *Gospel of Mary* and another (*Brucianus*) containing the *Books of Jeu*, also mentioned in *Pistis Sophia*, were acquired before the discovery of Nag Hammadi.

Thus, we face a multiple experience of what is *elsewhere*: historical and ecclesial, in the sense that it is not possible to go beyond the traces of such ancient communities; expressive, for the pervasive use of mythological and esoteric models that protect the experience of the group that expresses it, but at the same time excludes uninvolved readers; finally, for the intense spiritual journey that in any case they allow to reveal, elsewhere to which in different ways they all aspire. The *feminine* is involved in all the aspects just mentioned: Sophia is both the divine entity that caused the problem, and the equally divine resource that has given birth to the world and is at the same time every person who makes the journey back to salvation.

Moreover, these writings have preserved to a considerable extent a "memory of Mary Magdalene." Even from this point of view, it is not easy to discern how far they represent a traditional remnant that preserves a memory censored elsewhere and to what extent a reference of this kind to Mary may have contributed to her abandonment in other communities, similarly to what has been hypothesized regarding the identification between Sophia and the Holy Spirit. Finally, the texts are discursive practices in which the reference to women works according to recurring patterns: their presence emerges when a disturbance of the majority order is created and their mention is "transgressive or *infringive*." This term, deriving from *infringement* and typical of the law, is useful because it can signal a double point of view. Women infringe the patriarchal code and are pushed to the margins, contributing, in facts or in speech, to the marginalization of the countercultural system that instead welcomes them. Or, and this is the other point of view, they *disrupt* the homogeneity of the code and therefore allow them to narrate events differently. Women, in flesh and bone, are amid all this and constantly elsewhere: if the characteristics cannot be accurately reconstructed, we cannot eliminate them either, neither through silence nor omission, nor through symbolic reference, however sophisticated this may be.

Chapter 7

The Texts

A "Gospel" according to Mary?

The traces of an apocryphal memory of Mary Magdalene are scattered in the form of brief sayings or short stories in different writings, but they take on a very special importance in two Coptic texts, the *Gospel of Mary* (second century, in the Berlin Papyrus 8502) and *Pistis Sophia*, a generally used title of a long and complex manuscript (third century, the *Askewianus*). The two manuscripts come from Egypt, but not from Nag Hammadi, to which both the current version of the *Gospel of Thomas* and the *Gospel of Philip* (in the second manuscript), and the *Sophia of Jesus Christ* and the *Dialogue of the Savior* (in the third manuscript) must be traced, which also contain some mentions of Mary. The name of the apostle—alternating in the Greek between Mariamne and Mariham, both possible transliterations of the Hebrew name Miryam—is central also in the *Questions of Mary*, mentioned in the fourth century by Epiphanius of Salamis, in the section of the *Panarion* dedicated to the "Gnostics" (*Heresy* XXVI). All this leads, on the one hand, to the genre "dialogues of the Risen One with his male and female disciples," and, on the other hand, to the complex and discussed Gnostic milieu mentioned in the previous chapter.

In this context, the story concerning the *Acts of Philip* takes on a very special meaning: in a Greek recension, probably dating back to the fourth century in Asia Minor, there is a section in which Mary is a significant part of the apostolic group, together with Philip and Bartholomew, so much so that this text may well be part of the most important testimonies of a memory of Mary Magdalene. In the Coptic translation of the same text—or at least of the same model— she is replaced by Peter himself. In other writings, however, her memory is simply suppressed or replaced by Mary, the mother of Jesus, according to a process similar to the superimposition of all the figures of women in the Gospels (Gregory the Great, the *Homilies on the Gospels*, 33,1) or to the development of the Western tradition on the repentant sinner.

Other mentions, such as those contained in the *Gospel of Peter*, in the *Epistle of the Apostles*, and in the *Cycle of Pilate*, sometimes referred to as of *Nicodemus*, have another matrix and another map of diffusion.

All this data reveals a nonsecondary presence of Mary Magdalene, which reveals something of the communities that have referred to it and who do not belong to a single environment. However, the writings that most frequently transmit her memory offer a symbolic interpretation, at times spiritual and characterized by an evanescent sexuality to the point of immaturity, and at times of outrageous sensuality: a common destiny for female figures, especially if filtered through the male imagery.

Ann Graham Brox's study *Mary Magdalene the First Apostle: The Struggle for Authority* (Cambridge, MA: Harvard University Press, 2004) is an indispensable reference to the following notes. Then we should also mention Antti Marjanen's research, *The Woman Jesus Loved: Mary Magdalene in the Nag Hammadi Library and Related Documents* (Nag Hammadi and Manichaean Studies, Leiden: Brill, 1966), and François Bovon's "Mary Magdalene in the *Acts of Philip*," in *Which Mary? The Marys of the Early Christian Tradition* (Leiden: Brill, 2003, ed. F. Stanley Jones), 75–89. Along with the studies already mentioned in the first part by Marinella Perroni on pages 6–9 of this volume, they represent the bibliographic background of this study.

For the text of the apocryphal writings I mention throughout, I favor available Italian translations. I then give my own translation only for those texts not translated into Italian: in each paragraph, the edition of reference will be indicated.

THE GOSPEL ACCORDING TO MARY

In a circular or otherwise elliptical trajectory, it is not easy to identify a starting point. The apocryphal literature, as we have seen,

112

is at high risk, frequently shifting both as textual forms and as editorial epochs. It is therefore difficult to place the writings within traditions, that is, in historical contexts and in community practices, both regarding the time of their redaction and the subsequent stages of conservation and interpretation.

In the end, it seemed to me that the *Gospel according to Mary*[1] could be the starting point for this study. First, for the title, placed at the bottom of the text as frequently done in Coptic,[2] indicating that the text has as its own protagonist, Mary of Magdala. Then for how ancient it is: the papyrus code of Egyptian origin that contains it, called Berlin 8502 from the place where it is currently preserved, is from the fifth century, but in Egypt were also found Greek fragments, parallel to some passages of this same text[3] of the beginning of the third century, which makes the original text go back to the second century.[4] Finally, because it can represent a crossroads in Mary's multifaceted traditions: it develops the canonical theme of Mary's role at the resurrection; the subsequent *topos* of the dialogues of the Risen One with male and female disciples, and, in particular, that of the *Questions of Mary*, which also radiates in multiple directions, such as the Gnostic theogony, the conflict with Peter, and the mission in the world. Virtually all these elements are then variously arranged in the rest of the literature that I will examine.

The collection within which one can read the *Gospel of Mary* in its longer form, even though mutilated, is a manuscript acquired in Cairo in 1896 and then taken to Berlin. It is written entirely in the Coptic language of the Akhmim region, and the texts contained therein appear to be translations from the Greek. The section that interests us is included in an interesting sequence: *Gospel of Mary / Apocryphon of John / Sophia of Jesus Christ / Acts of Peter*. It is difficult to say the reasons for this choice in the absence of explicit explanations in this regard within the text itself. However, we can point out that the titles present three significant names: Mary, John, and Peter, respectively. If read, we can see that it has a narrative frame, with a text like the *Apocryphon of John* at the center, considered, as said earlier, as a kind of model/base of the Gnostic narration of the second century.

The narrative frame, if considered as a sort of historical development, begins with the dialogues of some disciples with the Risen One and ends with a part of the mission, that of Peter in Rome: in this sequence, can the *Gospel of Mary* represent the first step, therefore, the foundation of the mission, or of the old world, what is ultimately superseded by the logic of the *Acts of Peter*? Again, we are faced with questions that are likely to remain unanswered, but no less important.

The *Gospel according to Mary* (to use the form of the title) in the manuscript is arranged on nineteen leaves, but several of them are torn, so that the initial section, from 1 to 6, and a central section, from 11 to 14, is missing, and there is currently no possibility of filling this gap. Whoever reads it today is therefore introduced abruptly through a question, which, given the conditions of the manuscript, remains anonymous, on matter and its destiny, followed by a dialogue carried on by Peter on the origin of evil. An enigmatic answer from the Savior ends with the evangelical expression "he who has ears to hear, let him hear."

The next section, a remake of evangelical expressions, sees Mary enter the scene to support her companions. The sequence in fact begins with the Savior's leave:

> When the Blessed One had said this, he saluted them all, saying, "Peace be with you. Receive my peace unto yourselves. Beware that no one lead you astray saying Lo here or lo there! For the Son of Man is within you. Follow after Him! Those who seek Him will find Him. Go then and preach the gospel of the Kingdom. Do not lay down any rules beyond what I appointed you, and do not give a law like the lawgiver lest you be constrained by it." When He said this He departed.[5]

These words are followed by fear and sadness of the group, with respect to which Mary intervenes to comfort and invite to the mission and praise. Her intervention changes the inner disposition of her companions, who start to discuss the words of the Savior, until Peter himself asks her to expand on the teaching:

But they were grieved. They wept greatly, saying, "How shall we go to the Gentiles and preach the gospel of the Kingdom of the Son of Man? If they did not spare Him, how will they spare us?" Then Mary stood up, greeted them all, and said to her brethren, "Do not weep and do not grieve nor be irresolute, for His grace will be entirely with you and will protect you. But rather, let us praise His greatness, for He has prepared us and made us into Men." When Mary said this, she turned their hearts to the Good, and they began to discuss the words of the Savior. Peter said to Mary, "Sister we know that the Savior loved you more than the rest of woman. Tell us the words of the Savior which you remember which you know, but we do not, nor have we heard them." Mary answered and said, "What is hidden from you I will proclaim to you."

Thus begins the "revelation" attributed in its beginning to a vision that ends with "When Mary had said this, she fell silent, since it was to this point that the Savior had spoken with her." It is, however, within this section that a good three pages are missing: what remains, clearly fragmentary, nevertheless appears like a teaching on the journey of the soul through the passions and the powers to reach the upper, silent, spiritual place beyond time, season, aeon. Despite the brevity and incomplete state of all that remains, the context seems to be close to Gnostic teachings. The text then records the perplexity of the disciples with respect to that formulation, with Andrew as their spokesperson. The perplexity then becomes a clear aversion on the part of Peter, whose words, however, do not dwell on the form of the teaching, as Andrew seems to have done, but on the fact that a woman reveals it, which brings Mary to tears:

But Andrew answered and said to the brethren, "Say what you wish to say about what she has said. I at least do not believe that the Savior said this. For certainly these teachings are strange ideas." Peter answered and spoke concerning these same things. He questioned them about

115

the Savior: "Did He really speak privately with a woman and not openly to us? Are we to turn about and all listen to her? Did He prefer her to us?" Then Mary wept and said to Peter, "My brother Peter, what do you think? Do you think that I have thought this up myself in my heart, or that I am lying about the Savior?"

At this point, Levi enters the scene, whose mediation is interesting for many reasons, as he defends Mary and with her, explicitly, the experience of women, whose rejection is even attributed to the work of the adversaries; but at the same time, he also resumes the initial warning to not superimpose unnecessary frills on the words of the Savior:

> Levi answered and said to Peter, "Peter you have always been hot tempered. Now I see you contending against the woman like the adversaries. But if the Savior made her worthy, who are you indeed to reject her? Surely the Savior knows her very well. That is why He loved her more than us. Rather let us be ashamed and put on the perfect Man [see Eph 4:13], and separate as He commanded us and preach the gospel, not laying down any other rule or other law beyond what the Savior said." And when they heard this they began to go forth to proclaim and to preach. (*Gospel According to Mary*)[6]

The echoes of the figure of the *beloved disciple* are evident in the text: it does not appear to be far-fetched to say that according to this reading it is Mary the disciple whom Jesus loved more than all the others. There is also the baptismal idea of putting on the perfect man, a practically literal quote of the deutero-Pauline text addressed to the Ephesians (Eph 4:13). Moreover, Levi, which is the Hebrew name of Matthew according to the Gospel that bears his name, says something similar and at the same time dialectical with respect to the ending of Matthew 28:19–20: "Go therefore and make disciples of all nations…teaching them to obey everything that I have commanded you." This statement, as said earlier, forms an addition with the same expression at the beginning, even then attributed to Levi: Does it stage a controversy with a set of precepts attributed to the Savior that the authors of the text do not share? Is it just a traditional or archaic frame intended to capture a different kind of teaching, one that is openly Gnostic? It is practically impossible to answer given the absence of concrete references to the community behind this short text.

However, the strength and incisiveness of the statement remains that only the "adversaries" of the Gospel can deny that the woman is "worthy." This expression is very common in liturgical language, for example, it is present in the ancient eucharistic anaphoras ("I give You thanks that You have counted me, worthy of this day and this hour" [Prayer of Polycarp], "worthy to stand before you and to serve as your priests" [Anaphora of Hippolytus]), and in the rites of ordination/consecration, to this day: "Do you judge him to be worthy? After inquiry among the people of Christ and upon recommendation of those concerned with his training, I testify that he has been found worthy." In any case, the noun that derives from it in modern languages indicates the inalienable value of a person, better still, his or her dignity. And that is not a small thing.

MALE AND FEMALE DISCIPLES IN THE EARTHLY LIFE OF JESUS

Texts like the *Gospel according to Mary* are not interested in rehashing Jesus's life, even though the words that the Savior says come from the sayings that the canonical Gospels attribute to his teaching in Galilee. Conversely, others dedicate considerable space to it, and this is the case with two very particular texts, the *Gospel of Thomas* and the *Gospel of Philip*, both contained in the Nag Hammadi collection.[7] Both have interesting references to Mary Magdalene, placing her in the earthly story of Jesus. In this section, we will also briefly mention writings that, being very close to the canonical Gospels, recall Mary and her companions at the cross and the tomb, who will later become witnesses to the disciples.

The *Gospel of Thomas*

The *Gospel of Thomas* is an emblematic text from several points of view: it can now be read in Nag Hammadi's second manuscript (NHC II, 32:10–51, 28), introduced by the title: "*These are the hidden words that the living Jesus spoke, and that Didymus Judas Thomas wrote down.*" The manuscript, which can be materially dated to the fourth century, is preceded by the *Apocryphon of John* and followed by the *Gospel of Philip*, he *Hypostasis of the Archons, On Origins of the World*, the *Exegesis on the Soul*, and finally the *Book of Thomas the Contender*. The collection is the result of the mysterious community already mentioned, while the texts, at least some, are certainly older, even though in the absence of other witnesses it is difficult to say what changes have been made to the previous models.

The text that interests us here has no narrative form, as the canonical Gospels do, nor is it theogonic as the *Apocryphon of John*, but it is rather an anthology of *logiah*, that is, of Jesus's sayings, largely parallel to those found in the Synoptics, especially in the common parts of Matthew and Luke. The original language of the collection may have been Syriac or Greek: the first hypothesis is based on the presence of Semitisms preserved in the Coptic, and second, the proximity to some papyruses of the Oxyhynchus collection. The title, with the assertion that the sayings are "secret," is linked to the esoteric perspective that characterizes that environment, but the material that is collected is certainly older. It has been much studied, for example, also in relation to the hypothesis of the Q source. In minor proportions, a similar phenomenon is seen in a book from the beginning of the second century called the *Didache*: there is a section of sayings parallel but not identical to the Synoptic ones, while the general title is also later than the last redaction of the text, as it promises a teaching of the "twelve apostles" when the presence of apostles in it is never linked to the Twelve, and is nevertheless clearly secondary to that of the prophets. For both, however, one can think with sufficient plausibility about the evolution of a much older tradition, but it is impossible to go further and reconstruct a text that is devoid of the developments that are found in the present form.

The eponym of the writing is therefore Thomas *Didymus*. In the same manuscript, as mentioned earlier, there is also the *Book of Thomas the Contender*, which begins as follows:

> The secret sayings that the savior spoke to Judas Thomas which I, even I, Mathias, wrote down, while I was walking, listening to them speak with one another. The savior said, "Brother Thomas while you have time in the world, listen to me, and I will reveal to you the things you have pondered in your mind. Now, since it has been said that you are my twin and true companion, examine yourself, and learn who you are, in what way you exist, and how you will come to be."[8]

As we will see later, even in *Pistis Sophia*, Matthew, Thomas, and Philip (PS 42:3; 43:3) are the scribes of Jesus's sayings, while the disciples remembered by name are also others, both men and women, including Mary.

Thomas is presented as the one who among the disciples has an intimate understanding of Jesus. When in the *loghion* 13 the Savior asks to whom he is like, the disciples intervene in turn: "You are like a righteous angel," Simon Peter suggests; "You are like a wise philosopher," says Matthew. But Thomas replies, "Master, my mouth is wholly incapable of saying whom you are like." Then Jesus takes him aside, and then Thomas tells the others, "If I tell you one of the things which he told me, you will pick up stones and throw them at me; a fire will come out of the stones and burn you up." However, later he is no longer mentioned by name. James the Righteous is mentioned once, as the person to whom the disciples are to go (no. 12); Salome is recalled at no. 61, in a context of a certain importance, ending with her statement, "I am your disciple," which is followed by Jesus's assurance to her: "Therefore I say, if he is destroyed, he will be filled with light, but if he is divided, he will be filled with darkness."

Simon Peter and Mary are both remembered once in a distinct way (no. 13, mentioned earlier regarding Simon Peter) and then together in the saying of no. 114, which is also the end of the text. The first mention of Mary—without further specification—is no. 21, which is linked to the next through the theme of the "children." Given its importance, it is worth citing in full:

> Mary said to Jesus, "Whom are your disciples like?" He said, "They are like children who have settled in a field which is not theirs. When the owners of the field come, they will say, 'Let us have back our field.' They [will] undress in their presence in order to let them have back their field and to give it back to them. Therefore I say, if the owner of a house knows that the thief is coming, he will begin his vigil before he comes and will not let him dig through into his house of his domain to carry away his goods. You, then, be on your guard against the world. Arm yourselves with great strength lest the robbers find a way to come to you, for the difficulty which you expect will [surely] materialize. Let there be among you a man of understanding. When the grain ripened, he came quickly with his sickle in his hand and reaped it. Whoever has ears to hear, let him hear."

In the following saying (no. 22), the dialogue is between Jesus and the disciples, but starting from the children mentioned earlier, in response to Mary, it extends to the kingdom, declaring the overcoming of the antinomies:

> Jesus saw infants being suckled. He said to his disciples, "These infants being suckled are like those who enter the kingdom." They said to him, "Shall we then, as children, enter the kingdom?" Jesus said to them, "When you make the two one, and when you make the inside like the outside and the outside like the inside, and the above like the below, and when you make the male and the female one and the same, so that the male not be male nor the female female; and when you fashion eyes in the place of an eye, and a hand in place of a hand, and a foot in place of a foot, and a likeness in place of a likeness; then will you enter the kingdom."

As for most of the writing, the sequence of aphorisms, with a very similar basis to the Synoptic sayings but often accompanied by explanations that make them rather cryptic, does not allow for clarification of the background of this last statement, beyond a generic call for unification and combination of opposites. The "male not be male nor the female female," could refer to the baptismal expression of Galatians 3:28 but could also simply fit in with the other oppositions (above/below, inside/outside) as an overcoming of any form of dispersion and dualism. In light of these observations, however, the last *loghion* that opposes Simon Peter to Mary takes on further importance—in all the passages in which such a conflict appears it always follows this model, never in the opposite sense, that is, of Mary against Peter—explicitly mentioning the unworthiness of women and the need to overcome themselves by making themselves males:

> Simon Peter said to him, "Let Mary leave us, for women are not worthy of life." Jesus said, "I myself shall lead her in order to make her male, so that she too may become a living spirit resembling you males. For every woman who will make herself male will enter the kingdom of heaven." (no. 114)

No doubt, similar statements unsettle us today: it must be remembered, however, that Philo of Alexandria in the first century—closely followed by Gregory of Nyssa in the fourth century—commenting on the biblical passage of the Jewish midwives who let the males live contrary to the orders received, states that each and every one can give birth to oneself as a male, provided one chooses virtue, whereas on the contrary he will be female if he turns to vice (Gregory of Nyssa, *Life of Moses*, II, 3). Beyond the two authors as such, the recurrence of the theme shows how well established this gender taxonomy was, so widespread as to have appeared *normal* for centuries. The background of the *loghion* seems to be of this kind, because even in other writings in which similar expressions are found, they are related to spiritual dynamics and rational ability rather than to the rejection of sexuality. In this second sense, however, Clement of Alexandria (second century) shows that he knows a Gnostic view testified by the *Gospel according to the Egyptians.* The excerpt concerns a dialogue between Jesus and Salome:

> They are found, I believe, in the Gospel according to the Egyptians. They say that the Saviour himself said: "I came to destroy the works of the female," meaning by "female" desire, and by "works" birth and corruption....When Salome asked the Lord: "How long shall death hold sway?" he answered: "As long as you women bear children." (*Stromata* III, 9:63; 6:45)[9]

It is evident that this kind of reflection on what is proper to the *human* in the masculine and feminine form also captures the way in which the memory of Jesus and the group of those who follow and announce him is handed down.

The *Gospel of Philip*

In John's Gospel, Philip is mentioned several times and in at least three important contexts: before the multiplication of the loaves together with Andrew (John 6:5–9); again with Andrew, when some Greeks turn to him and Jesus interprets it as a sign of his imminent passion (John 12:20–22); and during the Last Supper, where he is said to have made the request, "Lord, show us the Father, and we will be satisfied" (John 14:8). In the Acts of Luke, besides the Philip who is one of the Twelve (Acts 1:13), there is also a Philip who is part of the seven chosen to serve as deacons (Acts 6:6), who is linked to the evangelization of Samaria and the Ethiopian eunuch, the conflict with Simon Magus, as well as the presence of the four daughters who had the gift of prophecy (Acts 8:1–40; 21:8–9). The subsequent tradition, however, does not distinguish the two, combining them in the idea of "apostle," and this is also the case with the *Gospel of Philip*, as it is titled at the bottom of the text of Codex II of the Nag Hammadi collection,[10] according to the use already seen in Thomas and in the *Gospel of Mary*.

The text is characterized by the esoteric form close to Gnostic teachings but also for its specificity as it speaks of five mysteries, that is, rites that in the West can be called *sacraments*: baptism, anointing, Eucharist, redemption (apolytrosis), nuptial mystery. On the occasion of the description of the kiss that the faithful exchange, the first mention appears of Mary Magdalene:

> The perfect conceive and give birth through a kiss. That is why we also kiss each other. We conceive from the grace within each other. Three women always walked with the master: Mary his mother, [his] sister, and Mary of Magdala, who is called his companion. For "Mary" is the name of his sister, his mother, and his companion. (*Gospel of Philip*, no. 59)[11]

The second passage is enclosed in a twofold sacramental reference to the Eucharist and baptism, and a passage in which one compares those who are to those who see. Mary Magdalene can be linked to both the sacramental themes, for the erotic reference can allude to the sacrament of the nuptial chamber, and to the image of who really sees, as it will often be in the *Pistis Sophia*. An epitaph in Greek found in Rome reads,

> You, who did yearn for the paternal light. Sister, spouse, my Sophe Anointed in the baths of Christ with everlasting holy oil, Hasten to gaze at the divine features of the aeons, The great Angel of the great council. The true Son; You entered the Bridal Chamber and deathless ascended. To the bosom of the Father.[12]

As we can see, the *symbolic* and *ritual* are interwoven with the anthropological and soteriological, so that it results in a text of great effect but not easy to interpret. In any case, even in the *Gospel of Philip*, a conflict is reported, albeit moderated with the other disciples, and resolved with a reply from Jesus worthy of the best Johannine irony:

> Wisdom, who is called barren, is the mother of the angels. The companion of the [savior] is Mary of Magdala. The [savior loved] her more than [all] the disciples, [and he] kissed her often on her [mouth]. The other [disciples]

[64]...said to him, "Why do you love her more than all of us?" The savior answered and said to them, "Why do I not love you like her?" (no. 63)

On the one hand, it seems difficult to deny that according to this version, Mary would be the beloved disciple of the Fourth Gospel; on the other hand, the erotic element that distinguishes the text binds it to the few details that Epiphanius takes from the *Questions of Mary*, all in that register, without it being easy—and perhaps not even possible—to distinguish the physical from the metaphorical.

The *Letter of the Apostles*, the *Gospel of Peter*, the *Acts of Pilate*, or the *Gospel of Nicodemus*

These texts I mention here in a synthetic way have no special development on Mary and her role, but since they mention her they cannot be completely overlooked. Two of them (the *Letter of the Apostles* and the *Gospel of Peter*) date back to the second century, while the third is a later text.

The *Letter of the Apostles*, written in Greek and generally anti-Gnostic, of the second century, has survived in Coptic and Ethiopian versions. The group of apostles is represented by the Twelve and Cephas is named last:

We, John, Thomas, Peter, Andrew, James, Philip, Bartholomew, Matthew, Nathanael, Judas Zelotes, and Cephas, write unto the churches of the east and the west, of the north and the south, the declaring and imparting unto you that which concerneth our Lord Jesus Christ: we do write according as we have seen and heard and touched him, after that he was risen from the dead: and how that he revealed unto us things mighty and wonderful and true. (no. 2)[13]

The women—Mary of Magdala, Martha and Sara, or Martha and her sister Mary in another recension—emerge at an important moment, but they are not part of the group asking questions, nor of the one preparing to announce the Gospel, despite the confidence that the Lord shows with women, so much as to go with them to bring out the fearful apostles:

> And as they mourned and wept, the Lord showed himself unto them and said to them: For whom weep ye? weep no more. I am he whom ye seek. But let one of you go to your brethren and say: Come ye, the Master is risen from the dead. Martha [Mary, *Eth.*] came and told us. We said unto her: What have we to do with thee, woman? He that is dead and buried, is it possible that he should live? And we believed her not that the Saviour was risen from the dead. (no. 10)

The same scene is repeated with Mary: no one believes her. Then the Lord decides to go in person, but he invites the women to go with him: "Let us go unto them. And he came and found us within [sitting veiled or fishing, *Eth.*], and called us out; but we thought that it was a phantom and believed not that it was the Lord" (no. 11).

The situation is reversed only when the Risen One recalls to Peter the episode of the cock's crow: this convinces them more than the word of the women. Significantly, the first of the unbelievers is Peter, and only in second order Thomas:

> But that ye may know that I am he, do thou, Peter, put thy finger into the print of the nails in mine hands, and thou also, Thomas, put thy finger into the wound of the spear in my side; but thou, Andrew, look on my feet and see whether they press the earth; for it is written in the prophet: A phantom of a devil maketh no footprint on the earth. (no. 11)

In the end they are sent on a mission and prepare to suffer the same reaction of disbelief that they had reserved for the women:

> But he said unto us: Go ye and preach unto the twelve tribes, and preach also unto the heathen, and to all the land of Israel from the east to the west and from the

125

south unto the north, and many shall believe on [me] the Son of God. But we said unto him: Lord, who will believe us, or hearken unto us, or [how shall we be able, *Eth.*] to teach the powers and signs and wonders which thou hast done? Then answered he and said to us: Go ye and preach the mercifulness of my Father, and that which he hath done through me will I myself do through you, for I am in you, and I will give you my peace, and I will give you a power of my spirit, that ye may prophesy to them unto life eternal. And unto the others also will I give my power, that they may teach the residue of the peoples. (no. 30)

The existence of a *Gospel of Peter*[14] was known to the historian Eusebius of Caesarea, who reports the extract of a letter from Bishop Serapion of Antioch (end of the second century) who had found it in use in a community, first approving it and later forbidding it. At present, there is a rather long passage known as the Akhmim Fragment, from the name of the place where it was found at the end of the nineteenth century, although it cannot be said that it is the same text Eusebius referred to.

In it, the passage concerning Mary and the other women is very brief, almost entirely parallel to the canonical tradition. The text is mainly remembered because in a certain sense it "describes" the resurrection, through the scene of two celestial beings who descend into the tomb and then go up again with a third being, going toward heaven, with a cross following them. A voice from heaven asks the cross, "Have you made proclamation to the fallen-asleep?' And an obeisance was heard from the cross, 'Yes.'" (nos. 39–42).[15] At dawn "of the Lord's Day Mary Magdalene, a female disciple of the Lord" with her women friends goes to the tomb and receives the announcement, "'Why have you come? Whom do you seek? Not that one who was crucified? He is risen and gone away... to there whence he was sent.' Then the women fled frightened" (nos. 50–57). Not entirely justified, however, is Graham Brox's observation according to which Peter in this case becomes the first witness to the resurrection at the expense of Mary: in reality, in the extant text it seems that even the soldiers who guarded the tomb and who witnessed the tomb are prominent witnesses, not Peter, even if in the end the apostle speaks in the first person.

The *Acts of Pilate*, also known as the *Gospel of Nicodemus*,[16] circulated widely in the West and became a model for iconography and the *laudi*, such as those of Jacopone da Todi. According to a recension—there are many different witnesses—under the cross to accompany Mary the mother of Jesus there were Mary Magdalene and Salome, who comfort and support her. The Magdalene, after Jesus's death, reveals her intention of going to Rome to Caesar to accuse Pilate. The *Letter of Pilate to Tiberius*, included in the same cycle, states that a woman came to Rome, the Magdalene in fact, to present to the Emperor a dossier of accusations about Pilate for his behavior toward Jesus.

THE *QUESTIONS OF THE DISCIPLES* OR THE *QUESTIONS OF MARY?*

Epiphanius, bishop of the late fourth century, recalls two writings called *Questions of Mary*, one short and the other longer (the *Greater Questions of Mary* and the *Lesser Questions of Mary*) in the context of a description of Gnosticism. From this patristic model, I present in the following pages also other writings in which Mary as a protagonist, or together with other male and female disciples, has the function of asking questions, in some cases even of advancing solutions and answers. A good part of *Pistis Sophia* would also be a part of this literary genre, but a special section will be dedicated to it due to its importance and length.

The *Greater* and *Lesser Questions of Mary*

Epiphanius of Salamis is a determined and unique collector of heresies: in the writing called *Panarion* he lists eighteen of them, as many as Solomon's concubines, giving the impression of altering a bit the numbers to reach the one he wanted. As is generally the case in writings of this kind, one cannot underestimate the lens of those who describe characters, movements, doctrines considered deviant from their own doctrinal and disciplinary system. However, even with such filters, much of the information is also very useful to grasp at least some traces of stigmatized realities, which also include many women, such as those of the Cataphrygian heresy (also known as Montanists), or the Arabian Colliridian heretics, who would offer sacred bread and cakes to the Virgin Mary. It may be significant to report an excerpt from the latter refutation because it can help to understand the general environment documented by the text:

> Who are there that teach such things apart from women? In very truth, women are a feeble race, untrustworthy and of mediocre intelligence. Once again we see that the Devil knows how to make women spew forth ridiculous teachings, as he has just succeeded in doing in the case of Quintilla, Maxima and Priscilla....Courage, servants of God, let us invest ourselves with all the qualities of men and put to flight this feminine madness. (*Panarion* 79:1–2)[17]

The question has to do with the entire project that we are undertaking here, and in this broader sense it will be taken up again in the final considerations. But it also deals specifically with the traditions of Mary Magdalene, because in heresy 26, in the context of the refutation of the Gnostics, Epiphanius does not spare himself in portraying them as libertines, accustomed to promiscuity and avid for eroticism. This is how the titles of the two writings are presented, even if the very short excerpt cannot represent the entire collection in the double recension that he had just reported. In this way, however, Mary Magdalene is squeezed in the general context of the accusations, as Epiphanius seems to be obsessed even in previous and subsequent passages with semen and menstrual blood:

> And they too have lots of books. They publish certain "Questions of Mary"; but others offer many books about the Ialdabaoth we spoke of, and in the name of Seth. They call others "Apocalypses of Adam" and have ventured to compose other Gospels in the names of the disciples, and are not ashamed to say that our Saviour and

Lord himself, Jesus Christ, revealed this obscenity. For in the so-called "Greater Questions of Mary"—there are also "Lesser" ones forged by them—they claim that he reveals it to her after taking her aside on the mountain, praying, producing a woman from his side, beginning to have sex with her, and then partaking of his emission, if you please, to show that "Thus we must do, that we may live." And when Mary was alarmed and fell to the ground, he raised her up and said to her, "O thou of little faith, wherefore didst thou doubt?" And they say that this is the meaning of the saying in the Gospel, "If I have told you earthly things and ye believe not, how shall ye believe the heavenly things?" and so of, "When ye see the Son of Man ascending up where he was before"—in other words, when you see the emission being partaken of where it came from. And when Christ said, "Except ye eat my flesh and drink my blood," and the disciples were disturbed and replied, "Who can hear this?" they say his saying was about the dirt. And this is why they were disturbed and fell away; they were not entirely stable yet, they say. (26:8:1–6)[18]

The text continues in the same tenor until it comes to the crimson cord that Rahab tied in the window (Josh 2:18), stating that it referred to menstrual blood. It is impossible to validate these statements. When in writings such as the *Gospel of Philip*, mentioned earlier, sacramental rites are discussed, the bridal chamber is also mentioned, but it is not easy to understand whether the rite actually included an experienced erotic dimension, or the reference was of a mystical kind, just as baptism is thought of as dying with Christ, or the Eucharist as eating flesh and drinking blood. It cannot be excluded, of course, in the absence of other proof, that there were similar moments in the actual rite, even more so if we compare the known elements with what is referred, for example, to tantrism, in which is important both the element of sexual union, and the presence of sexual fluids, especially male but also female, as an initiation into spiritual reality. It should, however, be noted, on the one hand, that in Epiphanius one of the recurrent accusations against the heretical groups has to do precisely with their promiscuity, and on the other hand, that most of the passages concerning Mary Magdalene in other writings, for example, in the Greek *Acts of Philip*, it is rather linked to the opposite, that is, to an encratic vision of abstinence from conjugal relations, of rejection of sexuality, and even of womanly appearance connected to it.

However, it is important to point out that there was a tradition with similar titles, also because in many other writings Mary asks questions: sometimes she is the protagonist; other times her questions are mixed with those of other disciples, thus giving life to an inclusive apostolic group.

The *Sophia of Jesus Christ* and the *Dialogue of the Savior*

The *Sophia of Jesus Christ*[19] has a good manuscript tradition: a copy is found in the Berlin Papyrus of 8502, together with the *Gospel of Mary*, and a copy in Code III of the Nag Hammadi collection, followed by the *Dialogue of the Savior*. A Greek fragment is also preserved among the Oxyrhynchus Papyri. This is the incipit of the longer text, coming from Nag Hammadi:

> After he rose from the dead, his twelve disciples and seven women continued to be his followers, and went to Galilee onto the mountain called "Divination and Joy."[20]

The first question is then asked by Philip, followed by those of Matthew, Mary, Bartholomew, and Thomas. Even Mary asks questions:

> Mary said to him: "Lord, then how will we know that?" The perfect Savior said: "Come [you] from invisible things...." Mary said to him: "Holy Lord, where did your disciples come from, and where are they going, and [what] should they do here?"

As you can see, the form and content of the questions do not isolate Mary, they simply place her together with the others in the "twelve plus seven" group, even though she is the only woman to speak.

The *Dialogue of the Savior* is a very corrupt text and therefore its reading is fragmentary. In it, the people with whom the Savior talks, however, are only three: he responds to them, for them he unlocks their understanding of salvation, on them he lays his hands to open their vision and to open their lips to praise. These are Matthew, Judas—often by commentators interpreted as Judas Thomas—and Mary. The three team up in asking questions and there is no conflict between them.

PISTIS SOPHIA

The use of the name *Pistis Sophia*[21] has been extended to include the content of a codex in Coptic language purchased in 1772 in London by an English collector before the discovery of Nag Hammadi. The manuscript is called Askewianus, from the name of the first owner (Askew), and cataloged as AD 5114 British Museum, from the place where it is currently preserved. It is now established to divide the entire content of the manuscript into four books for a total of 148 chapters, according to the scheme proposed by Schmidt in 1925. About one-fifth of the text consists of Greek words not translated into Coptic; among them is also the name of an important figure that is not present in all the sections in which the text can be subdivided, that is, *Pistis Sophia*. In the *Sophia of Jesus Christ*, previously mentioned, it is said,

> The perfect Savior said: "Son of Man consented with Sophia, his consort, and revealed a great androgynous light. His male name is designated 'Savior, Begetter of All Things.' His female name is designated 'All-Begettress Sophia.' Some call her 'Pistis.'"

This figure, which at the same time represents the divine entity that has transgressed, and the figure of the spiritual one pursuing its own path of purification, which understands from where it came from and reunites with at the place that would be her own, is named in the chapters from 28 to 82. Two phrases appear that could be fragments of titles: the "Second Book of *Pistis Sophia*" and "Part of the Books of the Savior," which are in the current second and third books respectively. The first section has no title, but its contents extend for much of the next, while the last (136–48) differs from the rest due to the different temporal collocation of the Risen One's speeches on the third day and not at the twelfth year since the resurrection.

All this is to say that at present the text is a compilation that combines several different works, but not simply placed one after the other, as in the codex that contains the *Gospel of Mary* (BG 8015), but intertwined and connected by the pattern of questions and answers that occur throughout. We cannot say whether such an operation could have been carried out by the translator or was already found in the previous Greek copy, but certainly it is not simply attributable to a copyist.

What specifically interests us here is the fact that Mary the disciple, sometimes also called the Magdalene, and in any case distinguished from Jesus's mother in passages where they both appear, appears throughout the entire compilation, representing in some sections the only person who asks questions and receives answers; in the sections where she is instead with other male and female disciples, she still is in a prominent position, both in terms of the number and quality of the interventions. A collection of this kind or the single parts from which it comes might well be referred to as the *Questions of Mary*. Certainly, this aspect is the only one that can bring them closer to the allusions of Epiphanius, because in none of the sequences does Mary perform sexual roles like those reported by the heresiologist. In fact, in Book IV, the writer states that he is aware of rituals that include the use of sperm and menstrual blood, but he clearly criticizes them.

It is not possible to report here in full Mary's sixty-seven interventions, which mainly have the function of allowing the presentation of the Savior's teaching, always exposed with the esoteric traits often highlighted and frequently parallel to expressions present in the canonical Gospels. For our purpose, it is enough to emphasize her presence in this tradition: either as the accomplished figure of Sophia or the beloved disciple, male or female, of the Fourth Gospel, her memory stands out among the other disciple figures mentioned in the text. I, therefore, will focus on three aspects, collected transversely and not according to the current order of the manuscript: the most frequent exchanges with questions and subsequent praise; the relationship characterized by both agreement and conflict that arise between her and Peter, which, as we have seen, are also present in other writings; and finally, one of the most original parts of the text, the hermeneutic and euchological probe of the repentances of *Pistis Sophia*, carried out in a sort of dialogue between male and female disciples.

The *Questions of Mary*: A Recurring Pattern

After a description of the ascension of Jesus, followed by his words of explanation, the questions begin, which are introduced by Mary:

> When then he had said this to his disciples, he said unto them: "Who hath ears to hear, let him hear." It came to pass then, when Mary had heard the Saviour say these words, that she gazed fixedly into the air for the space of an hour. She said: "My Lord, give commandment unto me to speak in openness." Mary Magdalene asketh and receiveth permission to speak. And Jesus, the compassionate, answered and said unto Mary: "Mary, thou blessed one, whom I will perfect in all mysteries of those of the height, discourse in openness, thou, whose heart is raised to the kingdom of heaven more than all thy brethren." (chap. 17)

Of great interest is the "linking" passage in chapter 83, which marks a passage in the path of return to the condition of salvation:

> It came to pass then again, after all this, that Mary came forward, adored the feet of Jesus and said: "My Lord, be not wroth with me, if I question thee, because we question concerning everything with precision and certainty. For thou hast said unto us aforetime: 'Seek that ye may find, and knock that it may be opened unto you. For every one who seeketh shall find, and to every one who

knocketh it shall be opened' [Matt 7:7–8, Luke 9:10].
Now, therefore, my Lord, who is it whom I shall seek, or
who is it at whom we shall knock? Or who rather is able
to give us the decision upon the words concerning which
we shall question thee?...Because we do not question in
the manner in which the men of the world question, but
because we question in the gnosis of the Height which
thou hast given unto us, and we question moreover in
the type of the excellent questioning which thou hast
taught us, that we may question therein." (83: 181–182)[22]

Later, the recurring form, especially in the part following the events
of *Pistis Sophia*, from 103 onward, in which the one who asks questions is almost exclusively Mary, is as follows:

Mary answered again and said: "My Lord, I will still continue to question thee. Now, therefore, my Lord, bear
with me questioning thee...." He said: "Well said, Mary,
thou spiritual and light-pure Mary. This is the solution of
the word." (chaps. 117–18)

An Inclusive Community, between Consensus and Conflict

It is above all, as said earlier, in the section 29–103, that of the
repentances of *Pistis Sophia*, that the interventions of male and
female disciples follow one another, staging a broad and inclusive
group. In fact, they are eight men and four women. Among the
latter, Mary still retains the main role, which in other sections she
retains alone, and is presented as the one who better understands
and interprets, the one that the other female disciples kiss to learn
skills and insights. The interpretations of the Lord's words are also
provided by other characters, for example, by John, who "kisses the
Lord's chest," or Salome, Martha, and also "Mary the Mother of
Jesus," the fourth woman of the group. Among the male disciples,
some have a particular role, that of "scribes," as we have already
mentioned in connection with the *Gospel of Philip*:

And when Jesus had finished saying these words, Philip started forward, held up and laid down the book in his hand,—for he is the scribe of all the discourses which Jesus spake, and of all of that which he did,—Philip then came forward and said unto him [... = he complains that he cannot interpret because he must always write]....
When Jesus had heard Philip, that he said unto him: "Hearken, Philip, blessed one, that I may discourse with thee; for it is thou and Thomas and Matthew on whom it is enjoined by the First Mystery to write all the discourses which I shall speak and [all which I shall] do, and all things which ye shall see. But as for thee, the number of the discourses which thou hast to write, is so far not yet completed. [...] in order that ye may bear witness to all things of the kingdom of heaven." (chap. 42)

Here, too, there are some conflicting moments in the interaction between Peter and Mary, but conflict is not the prevailing hermeneutic key, because in several cases the respective questions/ answers represent different hermeneutical levels and not opposing views, as can be seen also through the examination of the interpretations of Psalm 84 in the following paragraph. In the passage that we read now, for example, Peter, rather jealous, is presented while complaining about Mary, but is pitied by Jesus and affably invited to join the game of interpretations:

It came to pass then, when Jesus had finished speaking these words unto his disciples, that he said unto them: "Do ye understand in what manner I discourse with you?" And Peter started forward and said unto Jesus: "My Lord, we will not endure this woman, for she taketh the opportunity from us and hath let none of us speak, but she discourseth many times." And Jesus answered and said unto his disciples: "Let him in whom the power of his spirit shall seethe, so that he understandeth what I say, come forward and speak. But now, Peter, I see thy power in thee, that it understandeth the solution of the mystery of the repentance which Pistis Sophia hath uttered. Now, therefore, Peter, speak the thought of her repentance in the midst of thy brethren." (chap. 36)

Then Peter exposes, without receiving any reproach, the interpretation of Psalm 70. All of them offer interpretations that are accepted, and the conflict remains a little underdeveloped, emerging only occasionally. In any case, the text is aware of it, and whatever the way it resolves it, it is always in favor of Mary, never against her or to reproach her accentuated protagonism:

> Mary came forward and said: "My Lord, my mind is ever understanding, at every time to come forward and set forth the solution of the words which she hath uttered; but I am afraid of Peter, because he threatened me and hateth our sex." And when she had said this, the First Mystery said unto her: "Every one who shall be filled with the spirit of light to come forward and set forth the solution of what I say,—no one shall be able to prevent him. Now, therefore, O Mary, set forth then the solution of the words which Pistis Sophia hath uttered." (chap. 72)[23]

To some extent, Mary is a mirror of the path of recovery of the spiritual/sapiential dimension, which is the positive face of the ambivalent Sophia, and does not always find recognition. To what extent this map corresponds to a territory, as they say, that is, a real conflict between a genealogy (masculine?) of Peter and (feminine?) one of Mary, is a question that must be asked, but also left open. In any case, it is also a confrontation and a conflict around different, but equally intense, spiritualities, as can be seen in the kind of *lectio* that is displayed.

An Exegetical and Euchological Path

The most characteristic section is in fact the one that stages a sort of liturgical and community path, so that Sophia's story is primarily the path of her repentance/return, that is, the possibility for those who accept it to make the journey of illumination and liberation. Sophia has fallen, plunging into the world of mixture and *dissimilarity*, into a spiritual universe thus conceived:

(a)   the *ineffable God*;

(b)   around *him* three spaces of the first mystery;

(c)   the world of pure light/with three regions;

(d)   the thirteenth aeon + the world of twelve aeons (further divided into three regions) or "world of the mixture" of matter and light.

Misled by a false light, instead of being in her place in the thirteenth aeon, Pistis Sophia had thought of ascending without her companion to pure light and instead, without knowing it, she went down and fell into chaos. Then the path of awareness, repentance, and ascension begins:

> And Pistis Sophia cried out most exceedingly, she cried to the Light of lights which she had seen from the beginning, in which she had had faith, and uttered this repentance, saying thus: "O Light of lights, in whom I have had faith from the beginning, hearken now then, O Light, unto my repentance." (chap. 32)

Her path is marked by repentance (= conversions), explanations, and prayers. The prayers are represented by proper hymns, biblical psalms (quoted according to the Septuagint LXX), and the *Odes of Solomon*. This elaborate structure is presented through interventions, in turn, of male and female disciples who question Jesus, or propose solutions and prayers:

> It came to pass then, when Jesus had spoken [...] "Who hath ears to hear, let him hear." Mary again came forward and said: "My Lord, my indweller of light hath ears, [...] Thy light-power hath prophesied thereof aforetime through the prophet David in the sixty-eighth Psalm: 'Save me, O God, for the waters are come in even unto my soul. I sank, or am submerged, in the slime of the abyss,

and power was not. I have gone-down into the depths of the sea; a tempest hath submerged me.'" (chap. 33)

In this way, along with the twelve penitences, which mark the ascent through the levels (= aeons), twelve psalms are proposed:

O Light of lights, hearken unto me singing praises unto thee in the thirteenth aeon, my region out of which I have come down. Save me, O Light, in thy great mystery and forgive my transgression in thy forgiveness. (chap. 57)

The twelfth level involves the request for a "baptism": "And give unto me the baptism and forgive my sins and purify me from my transgression" (chap. 57), and accompanies the thirteenth penance, which is explained in the light of Psalm 50. This is how the passage to the thirteenth aeon takes place, which is a prolonged pause—at once transition, dwelling, and vocation to proceed further—encrypted through the ritual sign of the *wreath*. It is in this thirteenth station that a sort of *lectio* of multiple voices is introduced, followed by the "names of the Immortal," and then again an euchological structure made of psalms, *Odes of Solomon* (five), and six proper hymns.

Resuming what seems to be a ritual analysis, the passage to another level is marked by invocations calling for a double sign: from the twelfth to the thirteenth—baptize me!—and then at the beginning of the new path—"The Light hath become a wreath round" (chap. 59:1). The wreath, little or not used at all in the West, is frequent in the churches of the Syriac tradition and has an eschatological, staurological, and festive meaning, since it takes place both in baptism and marriage and is common in the lexicon of the *Odes of Solomon*.

The first intervention of the thirteenth aeon is Martha, who proposes Psalm 50 and is praised. Then Pistis Sophia proclaims a hymn, which ends thus: "Because I have had faith in the Light, I shall not be afraid; and the Light is my deliverer and I shall not fear" (chap. 58:9). Then Salome proposes an *Ode of Solomon*, the fifth, followed by another hymn, and then another explanation, this time by Mary the mother of Jesus, distinct from the other Mary, who presents an excerpt of the nineteenth *Ode* in which the wreath is also mentioned:[24]

> Then Mary, the mother of Jesus, came forward and said: "My son according to the world, my God and Saviour according to the height. [...] The Lord is on my head as a wreath, and I shall not depart from him. The wreath in truth is woven for me; and it hath caused thy twigs to sprout in me, since it is not like a dry crown that does not sprout. For it is not like unto a wreath withered that sprouteth not. But thou art alive on my head and thou hast sprouted upon me. Thy fruits are full and perfect, filled with thy salvation." (chap. 59)

The nineteenth *Ode*, of which only the first part is presented in the text, would continue to speak of *growth* and *nourishment* in God and of God, so that it can be read on several levels: on the level of intradivine reality, on that of the incarnation, and then from the point of view of salvation addressed to all through the milk, including a possible eucharistic reference. It is at this point that the ascent of *Pistis Sophia*—a new salvation—begins with a verse of interpretation taken from Psalm 84 (85):11–12:

> Grace and truth met together, and righteousness and peace kissed each other. Truth sprouted forth out of the earth, and righteousness looked down from heaven. (chap. 60:10–11)

In the interpretation of the verse, Mary Magdalene and Mary, the Mother of Jesus, follow one another, advancing explanations based on Jesus's historical events. Mary Magdalene begins, giving an overview of the descent of grace, truth, peace, and justice. Then Mary the Mother of Jesus recounts, with imaginative details, the childhood of Jesus, with the spirit who appears as his brother, identical to him, and is bound to the bed, and as soon as he is unloosed, Jesus approaches the spirit who "took thee in his arms and kissed thee, and thou also didst kiss him. Ye became one" (61:121). And then she explains the verse as referring to the incarnation through her and receives Jesus's praise.

Then the other Mary intervenes, who refers the verse to the baptism in the Jordan, and she is also praised, until Mary, Jesus's mother, proposes another interpretation: "Grace and truth met together,—it is I, Mary, thy mother, and Elizabeth, mother of John, whom I have met" (61:124). Jesus praises her by saying that now has been offered the interpretation "concerning which my light-power hath prophesied aforetime through the prophet David." At this point a section starts, the one with the names of the Immortal, to be repeated as a "sign" so that from now on "the Sons of God may be revealed from here on." The names attributed to the Immortal are "*aaa, ōōō*; and this is the name of the Voice, for the sake of which the Perfect Man hath set himself in motion: *iii.*" The explanation continues with a series of other letters, creating a sort of cryptographic mantra difficult to solve. At that point John intervenes, explaining the verse in a way that recalls the Prologue of the Fourth Gospel, interpreting *the mystery of mercy* as the unveiling of the *mysteries* of "thy Father, the First Mystery which looketh within" (63:127). This translation proposed by Moraldi may be close to John 1:18: "No one has ever seen God. It is God the only Son, who is close to the Father's heart, who has made him known."

A passage of this kind would have deserved an integral transcription, but a study like ours does not allow for it. I hope, however, that what is presented is enough to show not only the profound spirituality that runs through these words, even in their distance, but also the practical framework they presuppose, though unfortunately it is not easy to tell which communities and what communal moments they allude to. This fascinating and distant world that has emerged from the depths of Egypt also brings with it the secret of the concrete role of men and women in it, but at the same time it preserves at least a trace of it.

THE *ACTS OF PHILIP*:
THE GREEK AND COPTIC RECENSION

The last text we present is completely different, in terms of literary genre, language, and geographical origin. This diversity, as we already said at the beginning of this section on apocryphal literature, is very important, precisely because it allows us not to limit the memory of Mary Magdalene exclusively to the Gnostic circles of Egypt. At the same time, in the transition between the Greek version and the subsequent Coptic recension, there is a process of substitution of Mary that also deserves our attention.

The Greek text of the *Acts of Philip* is contained in its longer version in a manuscript of the fifteenth century found at the Monastery of Xenophontos on Mount Athos, which is a copy of an original that the editors date back to the fourth century.[25] Prior to the edition of this manuscript in 1975, a much shorter Greek version was known. In the Xenophontos version, the work consists of eleven itineraries, each named praxis (= act), to which is added the martyrdom of the evangelizers protagonists of the Acts 8—11: Philip, his sister Mariamne—one of the forms in which Aramaic name Myriam is rendered in Greek, and who can be identified with Mary Magdalene—and Bartholomew. We will examine this part of the text, not without following Bovon's observation, one of the editors, who links Mary's protagonism and the second part with the vision narrated in the first act. In the initial scene, in fact, a young man resurrected by Philip narrates the sufferings he saw inflicted on those who had slandered innocent believers. This scene narrated through the vision pattern can be read as a heavenly projection of the persecution that the marginal community undergoes.[26] On leaving the underworld, the young man in fact finds "an altar, and the celebrants of the altar were jealous men and from one to the other were steeped in hypocrisy" (*Act* 1.13).[27] The young man himself, who had been driven to slander by a she-dragon, had been punished for the harm done to innocent believers, identified as "eunuchs and virgins" (*Act* 1.10), according to the promonastic slant of the whole text, which decidedly reaches encratic peaks. In fact, the mother of the young man professes her faith by saying, "I believe in Jesus and in holy virginity" (*Act* 1.3). In a later passage, however, those who are slandered are also presented according to a ministerial typology:

> Michael said to me: "Leave it be, because these also blasphemed against male and female priests, eunuchs,

deacons, deaconesses, and virgins with lies about debauchery and adultery." (*Act* 1.12)

Worth noting is the fact that in the French translation, Frédéric Amsler lets himself be tempted by the normalizing form and translates *presbyters* and *elderly women*, but in the corresponding note he states that the Greek accusative is *prebyteros/presbytides*, observing that the latter might also be translated as "female priests."

It is then in the eighth act that Mariamne/Mary appears, who is presented as Philip's sister and remains part of the group, together with Bartholomew, until the last act and the martyrdom that follows. Philip is unhappy with the area of evangelization that has been entrusted to him, the land of the Greeks, and "grumbling he wept" (*Act* 8.2). Mariamne/Mary—"for she was the one who held the register of the regions [to be evangelized] and it was she who prepared the bread and the salt, and the breaking of the bread. Martha was the one who served the crowds and worked much" (ibid.)—spoke with the Savior and points out that Philip is distressed. According to a model already encountered in other writings, Mariamne/Mary, who is the one who understands, also has the function of consoling and encouraging. In this passage, her fortitude is opposed to Philip's fragility, staging a reversal of what is commonly attributed to male and female, a reversal that is also signaled by her masculine tunic:

> And the Savior said to her: "I know that you are good and manly in soul and blessed among women; and the woman's way of thinking has entered into Philip, but the masculine and manly way of thinking is in you. So go with him to every place he goes and keep encouraging him with love and much compassion." (*Act* 8.3)

To obviate the risk represented by the impetuous and irascible character of Philip, the apostle will be accompanied by Bartholomew and Mariamne/Mary in male clothes:

> But as for you, Mariamne, change your dress and outward appearance, and put off completely your feminine form and the summer garment with which you have

clothed yourself. Do not allow the hem of your garment
to drag on the ground, neither tie it up, but trim it with
scissors and walk together with your brother Philip. [...]
So you, Mariamne, see the poverty of Eve and be rich in
yourself. (*Act* 8.3)

The story develops through an interweaving of evangelical
teachings and signs of prodigious evangelization, in which fero-
cious animals are tamed and made human, evil and primordial
dragons are confronted, until the arrival in the house of pagan
Stachys in the fourteenth act. Stachys had been blind for forty years
because he had been devoted to the cult of the Viper; then he is
cured by Philip, who uses Mariamne/Mary's saliva for this purpose,
applying it on his eyes. Just at this point, some pages are missing
from the manuscript, and when the narration resumes, the scene
has changed and describes the city that converts and asks for baptism: Philip administers it to men, Mariamne/Mary to women
(14.9). In the following act, Nicanora, enters the scene; she is the
wife of the governor, whose eloquent name is Tyrannognophos. It
is Mariamne/Mary who evangelizes her, speaking with her in
Hebrew, the language that unites the two women, heals her from
physical illness, and convinces her to adopt sexual continence. Her
husband, outraged, has the whole apostolic group arrested. From
this episode develops the martyrdom, which has several moments:
all three are arrested, then Mariamne/Mary is stripped so that
everyone sees that she is not a man, but at that moment her appearance is transformed into a luminous form. Finally, only Philip is
crucified, while the *Acts* end with the continuation of the evangelizing effort: Bartholomew leaves for Lycaonia, and Mary to the
Jordan.

The narrative presents several interesting aspects: first, the
text is different from the cycles of dialogues of the Risen Christ that
we have examined so far and comes from other regions, demon-
strating a diffusion of the memory of Mary not restricted to the
Gnostic milieu. In addition, Mary plays an active evangelizing role,
without losing the initial role of the one who understands and com-
forts, but later she becomes a figure who prepares the eucharistic
liturgy, baptizes, and evangelizes. The general background of the

script is encratic, as it binds baptism to a choice of continence. It
also assumes that Mary Magdalene is opposed to Eve[28] and the
snake, but to do this she has to become masculine in appearance,
as she is already virile in her soul.

But our interest can only increase if we consider that these
Acts also exist in a Coptic version. In them, Mary disappears and is
replaced by Peter. As Graham Brox and Bovon observe, the Coptic
text is later; thus it becomes part of a strategy of removal and
replacement of Mary Magdalene from the contexts that see her in
the canonical Gospels, resumed, as we have seen, in various ways in
a remarkable range of other texts. In addition to this Coptic version
of the *Acts*, other writings must be remembered, first the *Revillout
Fragment* 14,[29] in which at the resurrection the same words that in
the canonical Gospels are addressed to Mary Magdalene are now
addressed to the Mother of Jesus:

> And she said to him with joy: "Rabbi, Master, my Lord,
> my God and my Son, you have risen!" And she came for-
> ward to embrace him and kiss him on his mouth, but he
> stopped her and begged her, saying: "Mother, do not
> touch me, wait a while because this is the dress given to
> me by the Father when he raised me, nothing carnal can
> touch me."

Even a Coptic homily, known as XX of the Pseudo-Cyril of
Jerusalem,[30] does something similar, and the same change of person is also in some passages by Ephrem the Syrian and Theodoret
of Cyr. However, we decided to trace here only the origin of the
substitution between the Magdalene and Jesus's mother without
having to multiply the patristic quotations in this regard. But it is
useful to remember another text, the *Questions of Bartholomew*, of
which there are Greek, Coptic, Paleoslavic, and Latin recensions
with considerable variants.[31] It reiterates the couple Mary–Peter,
but Mary this time is Jesus's mother, and not only is there no conflict between the two, but rather a race in mutual esteem, which
ends with the legitimization of Peter on the part of Mary:

And Peter said unto Mary: Thou that art highly favoured, entreat the Lord that he would reveal unto us the things that are in the heavens. And Mary said unto Peter: O stone hewn out of the rock, did not the Lord build his church upon thee? Go thou therefore first and ask him. Peter saith again: O tabernacle that art spread abroad. Mary saith: Thou art the image of Adam: was not he first formed and then Eve? Look upon the sun, that according to the likeness of Adam it is bright, and upon the moon, that because of the transgression of Eve it is full of clay. For God did place Adam in the east and Eve in the west, and appointed the lights that the sun should shine on the earth unto Adam in the east in his fiery chariots, and the moon in the west should give light unto Eve with a countenance like milk. And she defiled the commandment of the Lord. Therefore was the moon stained with clay [Lat. 2, is cloudy] and her light is not bright. [...] Peter saith unto Mary: Thou art she that hast brought to nought the transgression of Eve, changing it from shame into joy.[32]

Ann Graham Brox also reports a Coptic fragment kept in the Library of Paris, where after Jesus prevented his mother from touching him, he sends her to Peter and the others to give a good announcement. Peter welcomes her and blesses her. Then the Father (*sic!*; with the Son and the Holy Spirit) puts his hands on his head and consecrates him as "archbishop of the whole world."

At this point, again, it is unnecessary to multiply the quotations, since the countergenealogy obtained through the strategy of removal and substitution between the two Marys has already been highlighted, with the coinciding exaltation of the role of Peter.

A NOT-TOO-APOCRYPHAL ASSESSMENT

This survey of the apocryphal literature was, it seems to me, sufficient to show not only that the memory of Mary Magdalene has been kept alive, but also that it has crossed different geographical contexts and spiritual dimensions. Already an assessment of this kind is important because the quantity and variety contrast not only with the notion of Mary Magdalene's absence or irrelevance, but also with the subtler one of her presence in the Gnostic imaginary alone. The importance of such a context cannot be underestimated, nor the effect of the repulsion and suspicion, which, as already noted, it may have aroused in the other communities. There are, however, other considerations to make, beginning with the genealogy of Mary and of Thecla in a non-Gnostic context.

The first consideration concerns in fact a map of female presences in Asia Minor and Cappadocia, which in the *Acts of Philip* includes Mary, but is much wider. If we consider only one text or only the figure of Mary, we obtain an interesting but extremely partial result. But a diverse picture emerges if we also bring into focus the *Acts of Thecla* with their authorizing force; the testimonies of the second century concerning Phrygian prophetesses and prophets (= Montanists, new prophecy) who in the third century pass the baton to the traces of the prophetess of which Firmilian of Caesarea writes, who pronounces the rite of thanksgiving;[33] and the anti-Phrygian dossier reported by Epiphanius,[34] to include the *Dialogue of a Montanist with an Orthodox*[35] and the accusations that are addressed to the Euchites or Messalians.[36] The presence and the active role of women becomes an integral part of the dossier of accusations addressed to these groups, which at some point end up outside or at the extreme ends of the ecclesial community.

It is difficult to say whether there are women in these marginal groups because they are more open in this sense, or if the role played by the female presence has rather contributed to their own marginality, or if they are named to discredit the group considered heretical/schismatic, illustrating well "the rule of anthropocentric language, according to which women are mentioned only when the matter becomes problematic."[37]

However, it is precisely the difficulty of reconstructing more accurately the concrete connotations of the experiences we are talking about that helps to make the view on antiquity less approximate, which requires approaches that are aware of the complexity involved. And this is not just a matter of commemorative obsession: as it has been repeatedly observed, this question concerns contemporaneity, both in the sense of the authorizing force that the female genealogies have for today's women, and in the sense of the invitation not to seek a single reading or just one explanation of the phenomena, because it would never be adequate, even more so when gender perspectives are at stake.

A second consideration, which regards the emergence of a sexual point of view when speaking of female figures, refers to this same non-naive approach: in this case, as we have seen, the traditions of Mary are often relegated to this type of register, which portrays them in an erotic way or, conversely, an encratic way. In a purely abstract consideration, there would be no reason to reserve this register for women, as men are certainly not asexual; but a second rule of anthropocentric language might be coined: men move to a neutral register, while women, when they appear, disturb the aseptic nature of the scene, by introducing instinctual dynamics that deny the alleged neutrality of a context (which was a purely imaginary projection). This is true both in terms of the exaltation of eroticism and of its rejection: a good example is the *Acts of Peter*, in which his daughter becomes deformed and paralyzed, thus saving herself from the possibility of being asked in marriage! In the same sense, therefore, it is no surprise that in the Western imagination, Mary Magdalene can pass from apostle to prostitute, because the obsession is the same.

The last consideration directly concerns the *apocryphalization* of Mary, particularly evident when her figure is omitted or even replaced, by Peter or the other Mary, Jesus's mother, as we have seen. This dynamic is so strong, widespread, and persistent that it can also be found in a recent publication, in which there is no shadow of malice in this regard because there is not even awareness of the possible misrepresentation. I am referring to the *Gospel of Mary*, a concise volume that collects Pope Francis's writings, with the eloquent subtitle *For a Jubilee of Mercy* (Piemme, 2015, edited by Elena Inversetti). The cover copy clearly explains its position: "The protagonist of the story is Mary of Nazareth, the narrating voice is that of Pope Francis, for whom Mary is the key figure of that pedagogy of mercy to which the new jubilee is dedicated."

Nothing wrong here, since the name of Jesus's mother is Mary and in any case the Magdalene is not considered in the book, which consists of a series of reflections for several occasions, assembled by the editors; thus it cannot be either systematic nor complete. However, what remains is the conspicuous insinuation of a title that in absolute unawareness overlaps with that of the ancient text, to which it belongs by right, for precedence, and relevance.

Even these dynamics of invisibility of women are well known in our contemporary world, which, with our remembrance, we hope is perhaps a little less apocryphal, in the sense of inauthentic.

Conclusion

Thirteen are the moons in a year, that meet, always and
again in heaven, the full moon of the Easter of Liberation,
the Easter of Jesus, Christ, the One Who conquers death
and embraces our Life in His Resurrection....

Our patriarchal memory invites us to remember the
twelve sons of the patriarch, but Jacob also had a daughter,
whose name was Dinah. Silent and defiled, Dinah is Jacob's
thirteenth child and the official narratives do not keep
memory of her. (Gen. 34:1–2) Dinah, a woman silenced and
raped, as it very often happens to women, children, and the
poor in history, is there to remind us that there are not only
the twelve apostles, the foundation of the faith of our
Church, but also Mary Magdalene, apostle of the apostles,
faithfully present at the foot of Jesus' cross, and in her
memory there were also all the women who followed him
from Galilee (Matt 27:55–56) and that there, in the land of
the impoverished and impure, they saw him as risen.

Maria Soave Buscemi, *Le tredici lune* (The thirteen moons)

We have undertaken this journey hoping it could speak for itself, by
presenting a memory of inexhaustible authorizing force. In each
section and in all their developments there have been no lack of
assessments and clarifications: a thematic conclusion at this point
would be pleonastic and redundant. However, if we have started
this trajectory by recalling fairies, witches, and women hermits, we
can now end it with Maria Soave Buscemi's suggestion, recalling the
women and the impoverished of the world: regarding the narrative
about male and female apostles and how many they were, whatever
that number may be, we cannot forget that the number twelve is
fictitious, apocryphal, and the fruit of suppression. Jacob in fact,

did not have twelve children, but thirteen: Dinah, defiled and at times concealed by the narrative, emerges as a mother, a figure of Mary Magdalene, and many other women.

And, for us now, she is mother and sister of a tradition that can be truly inclusive, that can make room for everyone.

Notes

CHAPTER 1

1. S. Ephrem, *Commentaire de l'évangile concordant. Version arménienne,* ed. L. Leloir, Corpus Scriptorum Christianorum Orientalium 137 (Louvain: Peeters, 1953).

2. *Commentary on the Song of Songs,* 24–25.

3. For example, see Ambrose's long discussion of this question in *Expositio Evangelii Secundum Lucam,* X, PL 15, 1847.

4. See the bibliography of P. Thommes, "Memory and Re-vision: Mary Magdalene Research from 1975," in *Currents in Research, Biblical Studies* 6 (1998): 193–226. The Library of Congress has in its catalog 697 titles and the University of Innsbruck (Bildi) 211.

5. François Bovon, "Le privilège pascal de Marie–Madeleine," *New Testament Studies* 3 (1984): 50–62.

6. Martin Hengel, "Maria Magdalena und die Frauen als Zeugen," in *Abraham unser, Vater, Juden und Christen im Gespräch über die Bibel; Festschrift für Otto Michel zum 60. Geburstag,* ed. O. Betz, M. Hengel, and P. Schmidt (Leiden: Brill, 1963), 243–46.

7. Naples: D'Auria, 1992 (second ed. 1995, third ed. 2002).

8. Brescia: Queriniana, 1992.

9. *NTAbh* 40 (Munster: Aschendorff, 2002).

10. Freiburg: Herder, 2007.

11. New York: Paulist Press, 1995.

12. Biblische Gestalten 23 (Leipzig: Evangelische Verlagsanstalt, 2011).

13. Milan: Paoline, 2015.

14. E. Giannarelli, "La santa delle molteplici verità: viaggio intorno a Maria di Magdala," *Il riposo della Tenda* 34 (2009): 9–31.

15. Rome: Arkeios, 2006.

16. P. E. Dauzat, *L'invenzione di Maria Maddalena* (2006), 23 and 26.

17. Trapani: Il Pozzo di Giacobbe, 2012.

18. The series, planned for twenty volumes, comes out simultaneously in four languages (German, Spanish, English, and Italian) and represents a monumental critical history of women's exegesis in the Jewish and Christian traditions.

19. M. Perroni, *Il discepolato delle donne nel Vangelo di Luca. Un contributo all'ecclesiologia neotestamentaria,* excerpt from doctoral dissertation at the Pontificio Athenaeo S. Anselmi, Rome 1995.

20. M. Perroni, "L'annuncio pasquale alle/delle donne (Mc 1,1–8): alle origini della tradizione kerygmatica," in *Patrimonium fidei: traditionsgeschichtliches Verstehen am Ende? Festschrift Magnus Löhrer und Pius–Ramon Tragan,* ed. M. Perroni and E. Salmann, Studia Anselmiana 124 (Rome: Pontificio Ateneo S. Anselmo, 1997), 397–436; M. Perroni, "'Murió y fue sepultado.' La contribución de las discípulas de Jesús a la elaboracion de la fe en la resurreción," in *En el umbral. Muerte y Teología en perspectiva de mujeres, En clave de mujer,* ed. M. Navarro (Bilbao: Desclée de Brouwer, 2006), 147–80; M. Perroni, "Discepole, ma non apostole: l'opera di Luca," in *I Vangeli. Narrazioni e storia,* ed. M. Navarro and M. Perroni, La Bibbia e le donne, 4 (Trapani: Il Pozzo di Giacobbe, 2012), 175–212; M. Perroni, *Le donne di Galilea. Presenze femminili nella prima comunità cristiana* (Bologna: Dehoniane, 2015).

CHAPTER 2

1. Gregory the Great, *Homiliae in Evangelia,* book II, XXXIII, PL 76, 1978.

2. E. Giannarelli, "La santa delle molteplici verità: viaggio intorno a Maria di Magdala," *Il riposo della Tenda* 34 (2009): 9.

3. K. McGowan, *Il vangelo di Maria Maddalena* (Milan: Piemme, 2013).

4. The catalog of this exhibition is an eloquent testimony of the relationship among artistic representation, ideological convictions, and religious repercussions: M. Mosco, ed., *La Maddalena tra sacro e profano. Da Giotto a De Chirico,* Palazzo Pitti May 24–September 7, 1986, La Casa Usher, 1986. See also E. Fenu, *Mito, devozione e iconografia nella figura di Maria Maddalena fra Medioevo e Rinascimento* (Civitavecchia [Rome]: Abel Books, 2012).

5. Paris: Cerf, 2005.

6. *Commentary on the Song of Songs*, 24–25.

7. Hilary of Poitiers, *In Evangelium Matthaei Commentarius*, PL 9, 1844, 917–1078.

8. Ambrose, *De Isaac et Anima Liber Unus*, PL 14, 1806, 527–60; Ambrose, *De bono mortis*, PL 14, 1806, 567–96.

9. There is a useful, brief, but effective overview offered by Luz María Del Amo Horga, *María Magdalena, la "Apostola apostolorum,"* accessed October 4, 2018, http://dialnet.unirioja.es/servlet/articulo?codigo=2825169.

10. O. Roy, *La santa ignoranza. Religioni senza cultura* (Milan: Feltrinelli, 2009): "Holy ignorance consists of two things. The first is the devaluation of culture for the benefit of faith: for the new believers, in the worst-case scenario, culture only exists in the form of paganism and, at best, has no value, as for Benedict XVI, if not inhabited by faith. The second is the indifference to theology for the benefit of faith as 'lived.' In this case, holy ignorance is not a return to some archaism but the expression of a modern attitude."

11. On this, see E. Pace, *Una religiosità senza religioni. Spirito, mente, corpo nella cultura olistica contemporanea* (Naples: Guida, 2015).

12. The definition by D. Arasse is cited by P. E. Dauzat, *L'invenzione di Maria Maddalena* (2006), 20.

13. Jacopo da Varagine, the *Legenda aurea*, trans. William Granger Ryan as *The Golden Legend: Readings on the Saints*, vols. 1 and 2 (Princeton, NJ: Princeton University Press, 1995).

14. From a historical-critical point of view, a seminal work remains R. E. Brown, K. P. Donfried, and J. Reumann, *Peter in the New Testament: A Collaborative Assessment by Protestant and Roman Catholic Scholars* (Eugene, OR: Wipf and Stock, 2002). See also J. Gnilka, *Pietro e Roma. La figura di Pietro nei primi due secoli* (Brescia: Paideia, 2003); and J. P. Meier, *A Marginal Jew*, vol. 3, *Companions and Competitors* (New York: Doubleday, 2008).

15. An interesting, although partial contribution to clarify the role recognized by the Magdalene in the East and West is R. Infante, "Maria Maddalena tra Oriente e Occidente: Romano il Melode e Gregorio Magno," *Studia Antiqua et Archaeologica* 12 (2006): 187–98.

16. *Commentary on the Song of Songs*, 24–25. This title continues to be attributed to Mary of Magdala throughout the ancient tradition, from Augustine in his homilies, Rabanus Maurus, to Thomas Aquinas.

17. *Hymn*, 4, 40, 6.

18. Matt 27:56, 61; 28:1; Mark 15:40, 47; 16:1, 9; Luke 8:2; 24:10; John 19:25; 20:1, 18.

19. This is demonstrated with unambiguous clarity by the experience of Paul who, at the end of the 50s, recognizes that the community of Rome has enjoyed the apostolic effort of several women and that other churches in the area of the Pauline mission owe much to eminent women figures (see Rom 16).

20. Matt 26:71; Mark 14:67; Luke 18:37; 24:19; John 18:5, 7; 19:9; see Acts 3:6; 4:10; 22:8; 26:9.

21. M. R. Thompson, Mary of Magdala: Apostle and Leader (New York: Paulist Press, 1995), 32.

22. M. L. Rigato, "Maria la Maddalena. Ancora riflessioni su colei che fu chiamata la 'Resa–grande' (Lc 8,2; 24,10; Gv 20,1.10–17)," *Studia Patavina* 50 (2003): 727–52.

23. *Commentarium* series, 141.

24. *Epistles* 65.1. He calls her "turreted" again in *Ep.* 127.7.

25. For this and much more information on the archaeological research in Magdala, see S. De Luca, "La città ellenistico–romana di Magdala/Taricheae. Gli scavi del Magdala Project 2007 e 2008: relazione preliminare e prospettive di indagine," *Liber annuus* 59 (2009): 343–562. See also G. Paximadi and M. Fidanzio, eds., *Terra Sancta. Archeologia ed esegesi*, Atti dei convegni 2008–2010, ISCAB, Serie archeologica 1 (Lugano: Eurpress, 2013). Also see http://www.magdalaproject.org and http://www.regnumchristi.com.

26. This is the Magdala Open project for the enhancement of the archaeological site, which aims to favor the connection between archaeological interest, knowledge of the biblical data, and the existential dimension of the pilgrimage.

27. This expression is found in one of the texts of the ancient Christian pilgrims attributed to a certain Theodosius who, on the road from Tiberias to Capernaum in 530, says he came across the place "where Mary was born," precisely Magdala: see D. Baldi, *Enchiridion Locorum Sanctorum* (Jerusalem: Franciscanorum, 1935), 328–32.

28. The shallow waters of the lake have let the foundations of a tower emerge, a structure used for drying fish and to produce a popular sauce used by the Romans as a condiment.

29. From the excavations, a stretch of it—of eighty-three meters and precisely in Magdala—has emerged.

30. P. E. Dauzat, *L'invenzione di Maria Maddalena*, 26.

CHAPTER 3

1. See Matt 10:1–4; Mark 3:16, 19; Luke 6:12–16; and Acts 1:13.

2. Matt 17:1; 24:3; Mark 5:37; 9:2; 13:3; 14:33; Luke 8:51; 9:28; 21:7. See Gal 2:9.

3. According to some, there are four women because the mother of Joses would be a different person from the mother of James the younger.

4. The Greek text says, "When he was in Galilee" (οτε ἐν τῇ Γαλιλαίᾳ, 15:41). Matthew (27:55ff.) states that women followed Jesus from Galilee to Jerusalem (κολούθησαν...Διακονουσαι).

5. See also M. Navarro, "Discepole in Marco? Problematizzazione di un concetto," in *I vangeli. Narrazioni e storia*, ed. M. Navarro and M. Perroni, La Bibbia e le donne 4 (Trapani: Il Pozzo di Giacobbe, 2012), 149–73.

6. The question of the possibility of an itinerant women's discipleship is already posed in G. Theissen, *Sociologia del cristianesimo primitivo* (Genoa: Marietti, 1987). Later reproposed in G. Theissen, *Gesù e il suo movimento* (Turin: Claudiana, 2007). J. P. Meier is more skeptical: J. P. Meier, *A Marginal Jew*, vol. 3, *Companions and Competitors* (New York: Doubleday, 2008), 123.

7. On this, see Theissen's works (in previous note).

8. There are three (or, perhaps, four) at the crucifixion and two, instead, at the burial site and at the empty tomb (Mary of Magdala and "the other Mary").

9. See my essay "Ricche patrone o discepole di Gesù? (Lc 8,1–3). A proposito di Luca 'Evangelista di donne,'" in *"Lingue come il fuoco" (At 2,3). Scritti in onore di Mons. Carlo Ghidelli*, ed. G. De Virgilio and P. L. Ferrari (Rome: Studium, 2010), 199–211.

10. That Luke was aware of the involvement of wealthy women in the spread of the Christian proclamation can be seen also from Acts 17:12 (see 13:50) and the role of Lydia, a rich merchant of purple cloth.

11. Origen reports that Celsus mocks the faith of Christians in the crucifixion and resurrection of Jesus because it originates from the magical arts of a woman who behaves as if she's mad: *Contra Celsum*, book II, 55, PG 11, 1857, 883.

12. See 2:4; 7:30; 8:20; 12:23, 27; 13:1; 17:1; 19:27.

CHAPTER 4

1. See Matt 28:16–20; Luke 24:36–49 (Acts 1:3–11); John 20:19–23, 24–29.

2. Scholars agree almost unanimously that the Gospel ended with v. 8 and that vv. 9–16 were added later as the second ending.

3. Consider also David's words after the death of his son, born from the adulterous relationship with Bathsheba: "While the child was still alive, I fasted and wept; for I said, 'Who knows? The Lord may be gracious to me, and the child may live.' But now he is dead; why should I fast? Can I bring him back again? I shall go to him, but he will not return to me" (2 Sam 12:22–23).

4. See, for example, Jer 31:29ff.; Ezek 18:2.

5. Gen 3, but especially Rom 5:17ff.

6. Attested in Deut 25:5–10, this practice was however prohibited by Lev 18:16 and 20:21.

7. Paul also suffers the ridicule and derision by the Greeks of Athens (Acts 17:3) and must face the doubts of the Christians of Corinth regarding the resurrection of the dead. To them, in particular, Paul addresses the famous exclamation, "If there is no resurrection of the dead, then Christ has not been raised" (1 Cor 15:13).

8. Some fascinating pages on Rachel are in C. Charlier, *Le Matriarche. Sara, Rebecca, Rachele e Lea,* in "Schulim Vogelmann" 95 (Florence: Giuntina, 2002), 187–270. Even if only possibly, the opinion is still revealing that, precisely for this reason, Rachel, the "ewe," was venerated as the mother of the Jews in exile, while the sister Leah as the mother of the Jews of the Holy Land.

9. There are two traditions concerning Rachel's burial. The oldest is that it took place in Rama, a few kilometers north of Jerusalem, precisely on the border with Benjamin in Zelnach; a second, more recent, on which depends Matt 2:18, instead places Rachel's tomb south of Jerusalem, on the road to Bethlehem (see Gen 35:19; 48:7; 1 Sam 10:2).

10. Targum Neophyti, Gen 30:22.

11. *Quale Messia per le donne? Messianismi giudaici e cristologie proto–cristiane in prospettiva di genere: un probabile percorso storico–religioso,* ed. M. Navarro and M. Perroni, *I Vangeli. Narrazione e storia,* Il pozzo di Giacobbe (Trapani 2012), 107–24.

12. It could also recall the story of the transfiguration of Luke 9:28–36.

13. The use of the numeral as a noun and the determination it receives from the article make it clear that the primitive formula evokes the constitutive nucleus of the nascent community. We cannot here recall the broad debate on the historicity of the group of the Twelve. It is however now clear that the call of the disciples and the constitution of the group of the Twelve, even if its historicity is affirmed, must be understood in eschatological-apocalyptic terms and that the number twelve expresses the conviction of Jesus himself that he was sent to announce the kingdom of God to all of Israel. In other words, it refers to the new beginning of the eschatological era and has a symbolic and nonfunctional purpose, as it evokes the patriarchs to allude to the entire people.

14. Besides, that Paul himself had a broad understanding of apostolic service is clear from several elements: Paul never uses the term *Twelve*; he presents the apostolate in 1 Cor 12:28ff. as a charism, and declares openly in Rom 16:7 that Andronicus and Junia were ἐπίσημοι ἐν τοῖς ἀποστόλοις.

15. With respect to these four women, Paul uses a verb that has a well-defined place in the vocabulary of the apostle. The term κοπιάω (to work) refers directly to the missionary work, and Paul gives it a strong meaning when he refers it to himself (1 Cor 3:5–8; 15:10; Gal 4:11; Phil 2:16; 1 Thess 2:9; 3:5) and to other missionaries (1 Cor 3:8; 15:58; 16:16; 1 Thess 1:3; 5:12; Rom 16:6, 12). Compared to συνεργός (collaborator) and διάκονο (deacon), then, κόπος (work, fatigue) accentuates the laborious aspect of missionary work and specifies it as an activity that involves the whole existence (2 Cor 6:5; 11:23, 27; see 1 Cor 4:12). Even when he intends to postpone his apostolic work towards the communities he addresses, Paul uses the verbal form of the aorist (1 Cor 15:10 and Phil 2:16) or the perfect (Gal 4:11). He thus evokes his precise missionary activity of evangelization and the foundation of the communities. He does the same for Mary and for Persis. Could they have been both, therefore, among those missionaries who brought the Gospel to Rome? Particularly for Mary, it may be something more than a credible hypothesis, given the clarification with which Paul, as he does for himself regarding the Galatians (4:11), stresses that the missionary work of this woman was "among you" (εἰς ὑμᾶς; see Rom 16:6).

16. It is true that, when he wanted, Mark distinguishes between "brothers and sisters" (3:32), but this is a very particular case, given that

the reference is to the family of Jesus and appears only in some of the manuscripts.

17. Although already quite dated, the study by J. Schmitt, "Le Milieu littéraire de la 'Tradition' citée dans I Cor., XV, 3 b–5," in *Resurrexit*, ed. E. Dhanis, Actes du Symposium international sur la Résurrection de Jésus (Vatican City: Libreria Editrice Vaticana, 1974), 169–84, note 4, remains absolutely essential in order to focus on the literary characteristics of this unique kerygmatic formula, because it contains the most complete and well-constructed enunciation of faith of the whole NT.

18. A movie like *Judgment at Nuremberg* by Stanley Kramer comes to mind here. A drama about the Nuremberg Trials, with Spencer Tracy, Montgomery Clift, and Marlene Dietrich, the dramatic tension in it is dependent precisely on the awareness that the story is created by those who tell it, and those who tell it are the winners.

19. F. Bovon, "Le privilège pascal de Marie-Medeleine," *New Testament Studies* 30 (1984): 50–62.

20. Elisabeth Shüssler Fiorenza, *In Memory of Her: A Feminist Theological Reconstruction of Christian Origins* (New York: Crossroad, 1983).

21. This is a summary of chaps. 26—27 of the *De via beatae Mariae Magdalenae*, PL 112, 1878, 1471–78 (English translation: *The Life of Saint Mary Magdalene and of Her Sister Martha*, trans. David Mycoff [Kalamazoo, MI: Cistercian Publications, 1989], 72–74).

22. On the disruption of this passage and its consequences for the interpretation, see P. R. Tragan, "Il mattino di pasqua secondo Gv 20,1–18 Esegesi e teologia," in *Alla luce delle Scritture. Studi in onore di Giovanni Odasso*, ed. M. P. Scanu (Brescia: Paideia, 2013), 187–209.

23. On this topic, see Shüssler Fiorenza, *In Memory of Her*, 366.

24. R. E. Brown, *Giovanni: commento al vangelo spirituale*, Commentari e Studi Biblici (Cittadella: Assisi, 2005), 1269.

25. Even his specific presentation of Mary of Nazareth responds to the need to qualify her as a "disciple" more than as the mother of Jesus.

26. A. Rotondo, "Volti di donna nel Quarto Vangelo," *Annali di Studi Religiosi* 6 (2005): 287–305, at 288.

27. The story of the anointing of Bethany is present, in addition to John, in Mark and Matthew. Luke seems to know a different tradition than the other two Synoptics, in some aspects closer to John: an anointing

of the feet and not of the head; at the home of Simon the Pharisee and not of Simon the leper; about a different woman, a sinful one. It seems that the story of the sinful woman is, for Luke, interchangeable with that of the anointing of Bethany since the evangelist eliminates it from his narration of the passion. Once again, this requires us to ask ourselves what must have been the prescriptive attitude of the third evangelist about the discipleship of women in his community.

28. See M. L. Rigato, "Maria di Betania nella redazione giovannea," *Antonianum*, 66 (1991): 203–26.

29. See Ambrose, *Commentary of Saint Ambrose on the Gospel according to Saint Luke*, book X.161, in PL 15, 1866, 1937.

30. Thus F. Bovon, "Le privilège pascal de Marie-Medeleine," 51, who believes that, thanks to the skillful Johannine composition, the theme of rivalry emerges between the two disciples who run, with greater or lesser speed, toward the tomb.

31. W. Kasper, "La collaborazione tra uomini e donne nella Chiesa. Conferenza episcopale tedesca, assemblea plenaria," *Il regno. Documenti* 5 (2013): 166–75.

32. With it the pope "in the light of an uninterrupted tradition explained that the Church, on the model of Jesus Christ, has in no way the power to impart to women the sacrament of Order and that all believers in the Church must therefore respect this final decision."

33. He uses it only once in 13:6, while the term μαθητής (disciple) occurs more than seventy times.

CHAPTER 5

1. English translation: *Commentary of Saint Ambrose on the Gospel according to Saint Luke*, trans. Íde M. Ní Riain (Dublin: Halcyon Press in association with Elo Publications, 2001), 359.

2. F. Bovon, "Le privilège pascal de Marie–Madeleine," *New Testament Studies* 3 (1984): 56.

3. Ambrose, *Commentary of Saint Ambrose on the Gospel according to Saint Luke*, in PL 15, 1866, 359.

CHAPTER 6

1. The group is francophone and the acronym stands for Association pour l'étude de la littérature apocryphe chrétienne (https://wp.unil.ch/aelac/).

2. For example, what Jean-Yves Leloup proposes in *Il vangelo di Maria. Myriam di Magdala* (Milan: Servitium, 2011; original ed. 1997).

3. Pier Luigi Piovanelli, "Qu'est-ce qu'un "écrit apocryphe chrétien," et comment ça marche? Quelques suggestions pour une herméneutique apocryphe," in *Pierre Geoltrain, ou comment «faire l'histoire» des religions? Le chantier des «origines», les méthodes du doute et la conversation contemporaine entre les disciplines,* ed. Simon C. Mimouni and Isabelle Ullern-Weite (Turnhout: Brepols, 2006), 171–84.

4. Maria Zambrano, *La tomba di Antigone* (Milan: SE, 2014), 49–50 (original ed.: 1967).

5. Maria Zambrano, *Delirio e destino* (Milan: Raffaello Cortina, 2000), 275 (original ed.: 1989).

6. For the two quotes, I refer to Luisa Muraro, *Il dio delle donne* (Milan: Mondadori, 2003), 116, 118: "Most scholars (but not all) think that Plato invented it for his purposes. There is a group of scholars who do not even want to deal with the question, because they consider it 'futile,' that is not worthy of their attention. I am interested in it, because halfway between the documented historical existence and inexistence, in the midst of uncertain dates, professions without name, obscure legends, there are many women who interest me....The excluded fall into the category of absentee and we cannot in any way make them pass for nonexistent." For Mary Daly, I refer to Cristina Simonelli, "Il potere di nominare. Leggere Mary Daly fra i tempi," in *Un vulcano nel vulcano. Mary Daly e gli spostamenti della teologia,* ed. L. Tomassone (Cantalupa: Effatà, 2012), 93–105.

7. On Luke's tightening of the identification between apostles and the Twelve and, at the same time, putting Peter in the foreground, without dwelling on his betrayal, and in the background Mary Magdalene, see, along with the study of Marinella Perroni in this same volume, the cogent observations of Ann Graham Brock, *Mary Magdalene, The First Apostle: The Struggle for Authority,* Harvard Theological Studies 51 (Cambridge, MA: Harvard University Press, 2013).

8. Eusebius of Caesarea in *History of the Church* reports epistolary exchanges of the second century (Irenaeus of Lyons, Victor of Rome, Polycrates of Ephesus) on the date of the annual Easter, whose celebration in Asia was set on the fourteenth of Nisan, on the same day the Jewish community would celebrate Passover, according to a synthetic Johannine vision, while in Rome it was moved to the following Sunday. Both sides claim to refer to the tradition of the apostles, particularly that of John for the Asian side, which enumerates a quantity of "tombs," in response probably to a similar statement by Victor who will have boasted of the burial of Peter and Paul. Irenaeus, always "peaceful in name and in fact," affirms that "the diversity of the practice [of the pre-pascal fasting = of the date] confirmed the unity of the faith."

9. The reference here is to the initial lines, in which Tertullian rails against a woman—"that viper of the Cainite heresy"—who taught the irrelevance of baptism (*On Baptism*, 1:2). It is not easy to say who she was, but certainly she is not associated with the group who instead leans on the *Acts of Paul.*

10. Ugo Bianchi, ed., *Le origini dello gnosticismo* (Leiden: Brill, 1967), xx. The volume publishes the proceedings of the Messina Colloquium previously mentioned: http://www.gliscritti.it/approf/ 2007/saggi/gnostic261007.htm (English translation: Johannes Fabian, "An African Gnosis—for a Reconsideration of an Authoritative Definition," *History of Religions* 9, no. 1 [Aug. 1969]: 42).

CHAPTER 7

1. Luigi Moraldi, ed., *Vangelo di Maria*, in *Vangeli gnostici* (Milan: Adelphi, 1984), 23–26. It can also be read in the edition of Jean-Yves Leloup, who reads it in a spiritual and psychoanalytical key: Servitium, 2007. The text occupies pages 29–37.

2. The three words (*Gospel/ according to/ Mary*) are on three lines of page 19; according to the editors, they are the manuscript colophon.

3. That is the *Papyrus Oxyrhynchus* L 3525 at 9:5—10:14 and the *Payrus Rylands* 463 at 17:5–21; 18:5—19:5.

4. To evaluate these dates, we must remember that the most ancient complete recensions of the canonical Gospels are of the fourth century; earlier than that there are only papyri fragments.

5. English translation at http://gnosis.org/library/marygosp.htm.

6. The Greek fragment has the verb in the singular, and it could be interpreted in the sense that only Levi goes to announce the Gospel according to Mary. This possible interpretation does not coincide with that of the Coptic recension and in any case does not question the fact that the Gospel of Mary can be at the same time content of the announcement and title of the manuscript.

7. I refer here to the Italian edition edited by Luigi Moraldi, *Vangeli gnostici* (Milan: Adelfi, 1995), 3–20.

8. English translation by Thomas O. Lambdin at http://www.gnosis.org/naghamm/gthlamb.html.

9. English translation at http://www.earlychristianwritings.com/text/clement-stromata-book3-english.html.

10. I refer to the Italian edition edited by Moraldi, *Vangeli gnostici*, 3–20, 47–76.

11. English translation by Marvin Meyer at http://www.gnosis.org/naghamm/GPhilip-Meyer.html.

12. Luigi Moraldi, ed., *Testi gnostici* (Turin: UTET, 1982), 61. English translation at http://www.gnosticq.com/az.text/glos.af.html.

13. English translation at http://www.earlychristianwritings.com/text/apostolorum.html.

14. M. Grazia Mara, *Il vangelo di Pietro* (Bologna: EDB, 2002).

15. English translation at http://www.earlychristianwritings.com/text/gospelpeter-brown.html.

16. For translations of the recensions A and B, see Luigi Moraldi, ed., *Vangeli Apocrifi* (Casale Monferrato: Piemme, 1996), 153–286. Marcello Craveri, ed., *Lettera di Tiberio a Pilato*, in *I Vangeli apocrifi* (Turin, 1990), 368–400.

17. English translation at http://www.womenpriests.org/traditio/epiphan.asp.

18. The text (*Panarion* 26:8) is translated from the Greek edition, with facing Latin by Migne: PG 48, 343. In Italian, the publication of *Panarion* , ed. Domenico Ciarlo (Città Nuova, 2014) does not yet include the chapters in question, but chaps. 61—66; 67—73; 74—80. English translation at http://www.earlychristianwritings.com/questionsmary.html.

19. Luigi Moraldi, ed., *Testi gnostici* (Torino, 1982), 456–72. However, the entire Nag Hammadi collection is available in English translation at http://www.gnosis.org/naghamm.

20. English translation at http://www.gnosis.org/naghamm/sjc.html.

21. Luigi Moraldi, *Pistis Sophia* (Milan: Adelphi, 1999).

22. English translation at http://gnosis.org/library/pistis-sophia/ps088.htm.

23. Mary continues with the explanation of Psalm 29 (30):1–3.

24. *Ode* nineteen, also known in the Latin recension as reported by Lactantius, who applies it to the virginal conception, has a second part of great interest. See Cristina Simonelli, "Il Padre che allatta. La 19° Ode di Salomone," *Esperienza e Teologia* 7 (1998): 69–77.

25. Critical edition: François Bovon, Betrand Bouvier, and Frédéric Amsler, eds., *Acta Philippi. Textus, Corpus Christianorum Series Apocryphorum*, CCSA II (Turnhout: Brepols, 1999). French translation by Frédéric Amsler, for la Pleiade.

26. Similarly to what happens to the prophetic group in the *Ascension of Isaiah*.

27. English translation: *The Acts of Philip*, ed. François Bovon, trans. Christopher R. Matthews (Waco, TX: Baylor University Press, 2012), 36.

28. This combination is not so rare, even if it has had less fortune than the better known one of Eve-Mary: for example, in the mid-fourth century *Catechetical Homilies* of Cyril of Jerusalem, Mary Magdalene redeems Eve and her valiant faith (literally, virile) is opposed to the weakness and lack of courage of the soldiers.

29. *Frammenti copti*, in Moraldi, *Vangeli apocrifi*, 204.

30. Even these texts are commented on by Ann Graham Brock, *Mary Magdalene, The First Apostle: The Struggle for Authority*, Harvard Theological Studies 51 (Cambridge, MA: Harvard University Press, 2013), 127–42. On the homily of the Pseudo-Cyril, see Pseudo-Cyril of Jerusalem, *Omelie Copte sulla Passione, sulla Croce e sulla Vergine*, ed. Annarosa Campagnano (Milan: Cisalpino-Goliardica, 1980), 158–59.

31. *Vangelo di Bartolomeo*, in Moraldi, *Vangeli apocrifi*, 313–20.

32. English translation at http://gnosis.org/library/gosbart.htm.

33. *Epistle* 75.10.5 of Cyprian's collection: "ausa est ut invocatione non contemptibili sanctificare se panem et eucharistiam facere simularet."

34. To the Phrygians is dedicated heresy 48, to the "Quintillianists" heresy 49, another form in which the Phrygians develop, mainly in connection with Priscilla and Quintilla, thus indicating exponentially the presence of women as leaders of the movement (PG 42:855–82). Christine Trevett believes that this fact reveals a female presence even more

important than that of Montanus and therefore not limited to his initial group.

35. Anna Maria Berruto Martone, ed., *Dialogo di un montanista con un ortodosso*, Biblioteca patristica 34 (Bologna: EDB, 1999). In a singular way, the anonymous author states that the Montanist books written by women are evidently heretical, because for a woman to write is equivalent to praying bareheaded.

36. According to Timothy of Constantinople, they are destabilizing; they change the rules of orderly cohabitation. One of the claims is that they refuse to work; another is that the group consists of people of the most diverse ethnic backgrounds; another is that they subvert the most obvious rules: "They promote women as teachers of their heretic ideas allowing them to preside over not only men, but even priests. And putting women at their head they dishonor the true leader, Christ God" (*De iis qui ad ecclesiam accedunt* 18, PG 85:52).

37. Elizabeth Green, *Il vangelo secondo Paolo. Spunti per una lettura femminile (e non solo)* (Turin: Claudiana, 2009), 131.

Bibliography

SOURCES

Part I. An Apostle without a Story:
The Canonical Tradition

La Bibbia di Gerusalemme. Testo CEI. Bologna: Dehoniane, 2008.

Nestle, Eberhard, Erwin Nestle, Barbara Aland, et al., eds. *Novum Testamentum graece*. 28th ed. Stuttgart: Deutsche Bibelgesellsghaft, 2012.

Wansbrough, Henry, ed. *The New Jerusalem Bible*. New York: Doubleday, 2002.

Part II. An Apostle between Spirituality and Conflict:
The Apocryphal Tradition

The following are the translations and digital sources used for the apocryphal literature.

Selected Italian Translations

http://www.intratext.com/ita/.

Association pour l'étude de la littérature apocryphe chrétienne: http://www2.unil.ch/aelac/; http://wp.unil.ch/aelac/liens/.

Translations and Apocryphal Texts

Bovon, François, Betrand Bouvier, and Frédéric Amsler, eds. *Acta Philippi: Corpus christianorum, Serie Apocryphorum*. Turnhout: Brepols, 1999. For English translation of these texts, see François Bovon, Ann Graham Brock, and Christopher R. Matthews, eds. *The Apocryphal Acts of the Apostles: Harvard Divinity School Studies*.

Cambridge, MA: Harvard University Center for the Study of World Religions, 1999.

Craveri, Marcello, ed. *Lettera di Tiberio a Pilato*. In *I Vangeli apocrifi*. Turin: Einaudi, 1990.

Grazia Mara, Maria. *Vangelo di Pietro*. Bologna: EDB, 2002.

Moraldi, Luigi, ed. *Pistis Sophia*. Milan: Adelphi, 1999.

———. *Testi gnostici*. Turin: UTET, 1982. English translation of the Nag Hammadi collection at http://www.gnosis.org/naghamm.

———. *Vangeli Apocrifi*. Casale Monferrato: Piemme, 1996.

———. *Vangeli gnostici: Vangeli di Tomaso, Maria, Verità, Filippo*. Milan: Adelphi, 1984.

STUDIES

Given the vast bibliography on the subject, we limit ourselves to reporting only the studies to which, directly or indirectly, we have referred.

Part I. An Apostle without a Story: The Canonical Tradition

Bovon, François. "Le privilège pascal de Marie-Madeleine." *New Testament Studies* 30 (1984): 50–62.

Dauzat, Pierre-Emanuel. *L'invenzione di Maria Maddalena*. Rome: Arkeios, 2006.

Giannarelli, Elena. "La santa dalle molteplici identità: viaggio intorno a Maria di Magdala." *Il riposo della Tenda* 34 (2009): 9–31.

Hengel, Martin. "Maria Magdalena und die Frauen als Zeugen." In *Abraham unser Vater. Juden und Christen im Gespräch über die Bibel* (FSO. Michel), edited by O. Betz, M. Hengel, and P. Schmidt, 243–56. Cologne: Leiden, 1963.

Navarro Puerto, Mercedes. "Discepole in Marco? Problematizzazione di un concetto." In *I Vangeli. Narrazioni e storia*, edited by M. Navarro and M. Perroni, 151–75. La Bibbia e le donne 4. Trapani: Il Pozzo di Giacobbe, 2012.

Perroni, Marinella. "Discepole, ma non apostole: l'opera di Luca." In *I Vangeli. Narrazioni e storia*, edited by M. Navarro and M. Perroni,

175–212. La Bibbia e le donne 4. Trapani: Il Pozzo di Giacobbe, 2012.

———. "Il discepolato delle donne nel Vangelo di Luca. Un contributo all'ecclesiologia neotestamentaria." Excerpt from PhD diss., the Pontifical College of Sant'Anselmo, Rome, 1995.

———. "L'annuncio pasquale alle/delle donne (Mc 1, 1–8): alle origini della tradizione kerygmatica." In *Patrimonium fidei: traditionsgeschichtliches Verstehen am Ende? Festschrift für Magnus Löhrer und Pius–Ramon Tragan,* edited by M. Perroni and E. Salmann, 397–436. Studia Anselmiana 124. Pontificio Ateneo S. Anselmo, Rome 1997.

———. *Le donne di Galilea. Presenze femminili nella prima comunità Cristiana.* Bologna: Dehoniane, 2015.

———. "'Muriò y fue sepultado.' La contribución de las discípulas de Jesús a la elaboracion de la fe en la resurreción." In *En el umbral. Muerte y Teología en perspectíva de mujeres, En clave de mujer,* edited by M. Navarro, 147–80. Bilbao: Desclée de Brouwer, 2006.

———. "Ricche patrone o discepole di Gesù? (Lc 8,1–3). A proposito di Luca 'Evangelista delle donne.'" In *"Lingue come di fuoco" (At 2,3). Scritti lucani in onore di Mons. Carlo Ghidelli,* edited by G. De Virgilio and P. L. Ferrari, 199–211. Rome: Studium, 2010.

Petersen, Silke. *Maria aus Magdala. Die Jüngerin, die Jesus liebte.* Biblische Gestalten 23. Leipzig: Evangelische Verlagsanstalt, 2011.

Ricci, Carla. *Maria di Magdala e le molte altre. Donne sul cammino di Gesù.* Naples: D'Auria, 1991 [2/1995, 3/2002].

Rotondo, Arianna. "Volti di donna nel Quarto Vangelo." *Annali di Studi Religiosi* 6 (2005): 287–305.

Ruschmann, Susanne. *Maria von Magdala: Jüngerin, Apostolin, Glaubensvorbild.* NTAbh 40. Münster: AschendorV, 2002.

Sebastiani, Lilia. *Transfigurazione. Il personaggio evangelico di Maria di Magdala e il mito della peccatrice nella tradizione occidentale.* Brescia: Queriniana, 1992.

Taschl-Erber, Andrea. *Maria von Magdalaerste Apostolin? Joh 20,1–18, in Tradition und Relecture.* Freiburg: Herder, 2007.

Thompson, Mary R. *Mary of Magdala: Apostle and Leader.* Mahwah, NJ: Paulist Press, 1995.

Part II. An Apostle between Spirituality and Conflict: The Apocryphal Tradition

Bianchi, Ugo, ed. *Le origini dello gnosticismo.* Leiden: Brill, 1967 (see http://www.gliscritti.it/approf/2007/saggi/.htm).

Bovon, François. "Mary Magdalene in the *Acts of Philip.*" In *Which Mary? The Marys of the Early Christian Tradition*, edited by F. Stanley Jones, 75–89. Leiden: Brill, 2003.

Graham Brock, Ann. *Mary Magdalene, the First Apostle: The Struggle for Authority.* Harvard Theological Studies 51. Cambridge, MA: Harvard University Press, 2013.

Green, Elizabeth. *Il vangelo secondo Paolo. Spunti per una lettura femminile (e non solo).* Turin: Claudiana, 2009.

Leloup, Jean-Ives. *Il vangelo di Maria. Myriam di Magdala.* Milan: Servitium, 2011 (1st ed.: 1997).

Marjanen, Antri. *The Woman Jesus Loved: Mary Magdalene in the Nag Hammadi Library and Related Documents.* Nag Hammadi and Manichaean Studies 40. Leiden: Brill, 1996.

Muraro, Luisa. *Il dio delle donne.* Milan: Mondadori, 2003.

Piovanelli, Pierluigi. "Qu'est-ce qu'un 'écrit apochryphe chrétien,' et comment ça marche? Quelques suggestions pour une herméneutique apochryphe." In *Pierre Geoltrain, ou Comment faire "l'histoire" des religions? Le chantier des "origines," les méthodes du doute et la conversation contemporaine entre les disciplines*, edited by Simon C. Minouni and Isabelle Ullern-Weité, 171–84. Turnhout: Brepols, 2006.

Jones, Stanley F., ed. *Which Mary? The Marys of the Early Christian Tradition.* Leiden: Brill, 2003.

Tomassone, Letizia, ed. *Un vulcano nel vulcano. Mary Daly e gli spostamenti della teologia.* Cantalupa (Turin): Effatà, 2012.

Trevett, Christine. *Montanism: Gender, Authority and the New Prophecy.* Cambridge: Cambridge University Press, 1996.

Zambrano, Maria. *Delirio e destino.* Milan: Raffaello Cortina, 2000 (1st ed.: 1989).

———. *La tomba di Antigone.* Milan: SE, 2014 (1st ed.: 1967).